CW00996416

# *SEASON*
# *of*
# *GOODWILL*

By

Thelma Coster

Published by

**MELROSE BOOKS**

An Imprint of Melrose Press Limited
St Thomas Place, Ely
Cambridgeshire
CB7 4GG, UK
www.melrosebooks.co.uk

**FIRST EDITION**

Cover designed by Hannah Belcher

**ISBN 978-1-907732-98-0**

Printed and bound in Great Britain by:
Mimeo Ltd, Huntingdon, Cambridgeshire

FSC
www.fsc.org
MIX
From responsible
sources
FSC® C019549

## Acknowledgements

With thanks to my wonderful late husband,
for his support and encouragement in every project I have ever
undertaken.
It was his idea that I write this book, and for that I am ever grateful.

A special thank you, too, to a dear friend who stood by me through
thick and thin, and who took on the task of typing and proof-reading
this work, offering advice and guidance as she tirelessly edited and
amended. Thanks Polly, you are a star. Without you, Ron's wish
would never have reached fruition.

# CONTENTS

# INTRODUCTION

The Season of Goodwill is, for many families, one of the most stressful times of the year. Alongside divorce, moving house and the death of a loved one or close friend, Christmas is one of the chief causes of depression, stress and family breakdown. Statistics attest to high divorce rates and family break-ups at this time, which is hardly surprising given the pressures of not only catering for a long holiday, together with the cost of seasonal food, drink and expensive presents, but also the debts incurred as a result, which often take months to pay off.

Mixing with in-laws, family members, and particularly the extended family members who are not normally around on a day-to-day basis, can create additional difficulties, and must, in my opinion, be every mother's worst nightmare. Fractious children, distant relatives, relations who don't get on, partners who don't pull their weight, and the resulting arguments, put additional pressures on mums (and other heads of households responsible for entertaining others) to keep things running smoothly, and restore or attempt to keep the peace.

Young children don't like having their routines upset, elderly relatives don't like noise, and keeping a balance is very difficult. Unless you are the world's best caterer and used to cooking for large numbers of people all year round, the preparation and cooking of Christmas dinner can be a trauma in itself, and should not be undertaken lightly.

As far as gifts and presents are concerned, everyone seems to expect Santa to provide exactly what they have asked for, irrespective of cost. For some reason, concern about purchasing beyond affordable levels and the resulting consequences, common sense and good financial management all seem to fly out of the window, just 'because it's Christmas'.

It is no wonder then that many people approach this time of year with a sense of dread. Perhaps, having suffered bad experiences at this time in the past, feelings of dislike for Christmas are further intensified for some people.

Some people actually enjoy Christmas and love it, along with the family gatherings and the festivities. To those I say, 'Brilliant, well done, enjoy it.' There are those who would like Christmas to last all year round—again I say, fine. Such people, however, are a minority. Christmas just isn't for me. I personally know of many families and friends who have been split apart over the Christmas period, either before, during or after the festivities, and the resulting devastation and disbelief has caused serious long-term effects on many of those involved.

This book, *Season of Goodwill*, is one woman's story of the trauma that has followed her through life, and continues to do so at every 'Season of Goodwill'.

~~~~~~~~~~~~~~~~~~~~~~~~

# PROLOGUE
## August

It was one of those lovely, balmy summer days. The sky was blue, not a cloud was in sight, and the air was warm and fresh. It was one of those days when you feel that all is right with the world. I felt light-hearted and joyful, and there was a spring in my step. Wearing a light cotton crochet top, loose silky navy trousers and cross-strapped, low-heeled sandals, I felt relaxed and happy.

I had parked the car in an out-of-town-centre car park after dropping off my husband at a large DIY store, and walked through the maze of back streets leading to the town centre and high street shops.

Passing through the Granary building walkway (a lovely old building housing a restaurant, public house and a few small specialist shops), over the new red and black brick bridge, I glanced at the baby ducklings swimming behind a pair of mallards, and a pair of graceful swans heading towards me, just gliding along on the still, murky waters towards the bridge. Being close to the coast the river takes on a different look depending on the tide, and when it is high tide the water is high enough to cover all the rubbish which would otherwise be visible on the muddy bottom and the steep banks. At low tide the rusting cans, discarded supermarket trolleys, glass bottles and other trash make for an unpleasant view! Today it looked cleaner than usual and the sunlight made the ripples sparkle.

No one would ever guess that this place was once the greatest fishing port in the world and centre of the fishing industry. Now, there is no smell of fish, and a considerably reduced fishing fleet. The few remaining boats anchored along the quay are all that is left of a once thriving industry. But, the town is still a fishing centre. It has a rich, local history and an impressive Fishing Heritage Museum to be proud of, with the *Ross Tiger* fishing vessel moored alongside, where a cheerful skipper will give an absolutely delightful, funny and moving running commentary of life at sea for a fisherman.

Permanently moored boats house restaurants, bars and nightclubs, and the quay and docks are still extremely busy. The market and shops display no link to the area's fishing port history, although there is a wealth of really good fish and chip shops and restaurants around.

A major feature of the town is that it is surrounded by beautiful countryside, with the Yorkshire Wolds to the north and Lincolnshire Wolds to the south. A wonderful suspension bridge spans the Humber River, and there is easy access to miles of sandy beaches and numerous leisure facilities.

It is a beautiful area in which to live. The Seal Sanctuary at Donna Nook is a delight to visit, especially when the baby seals are born. The area encompasses miles of good walks, the Viking Way, and wildlife and bird life are in abundance, with sanctuaries and migration points along the coast. The pace of life is slow and easy.

On approaching the pedestrian crossing, even the traffic seemed calmer and quieter today. As the lights changed and the green man lit up to the bleeps, I crossed the road into the shadow of the outer wall of the indoor shopping mall. The tedious chore of shopping couldn't dampen my spirits today and, pulling back the heavy glass door, I entered the cavernous foyer to a blare of thumping pop music which resonated around the whole area, polluting the atmosphere with its dreadful din.

This enormous building had been completed ten years earlier, after a mass clearance of old and derelict shops, to bring the town centre and high street up to date and prepare the local people for shopping in the twenty-first century, which was now only a few months away.

The domed entrance foyer was like a sector of a modern cathedral with a high, glazed, panelled roof from which large glass ball lights were suspended at intervals from end to end, and red brick walls with pointed windows graced the far end. An interesting plaque halfway along the wall indicated finds during the demolition and excavation when preparing the site for the new development. People often stopped at this point to reflect on the plaque, which read, 'Site of Austin Friary circa 1293–1539. Some human remains from the medieval monastery have been reburied in Scartho Road Cemetery'.

Passing through the second set of swing doors at the far end into the open airy shopping mall, the blare of music dimmed to a gentler lull. Surrounded now with the hum of chatter and laughter, the to-ing and fro-ing of shoppers, and security guards talking into hand-held radios, the music faded into the background. There was the usual activity around the information desk and the general working buzz within the complex. I looked into my handbag for my prepared list and planned a route around the shops.

The shopping mall seemed extra busy today. Everyone appeared to be out to make the most of the gorgeous weather and here I was, in a shopping mall not dissimilar to the one I had left behind when moving to Lincolnshire, but feeling far more at home here.

We had moved from a very busy town providing both employment and housing, for which we were delighted while we needed it, but it took between twenty and thirty minutes to travel three miles to work by car due to the rush hour congestion. Everywhere in that Essex town the car parks were always full, cars are parked on both sides of the streets, and people and noise were ever present!

Since moving away eleven years earlier from the rat race of the industrial southeastern corner of England into a rural village, neither my husband nor I had ever regretted the change of lifestyle, and had come to love this fresher, cleaner, freer and slower way of life. It suited us both and we felt much better, in both health and temperament.

It took four years to discover this beautiful area of England to which we finally moved, where a traffic jam constituted a mere two cars behind a tractor. The village we chose is central to three towns: the fishing port of Grimsby fifteen miles to the north, the run-down market town of Market Rasen with its own racecourse lay eight miles to the west, and the lovely old historic market town of Louth was just ten miles away. All this was set in a picturesque wold area ideal for walking and surrounded by lots of places full of historical interest, such as a cathedral city only half an hour's drive away, and the coast ten miles as the crow flies. My husband and I often marvelled at our luck in finding such an idyllic place to live.

After my initial visit to the Lottery shop for the weekly £1 gamble I allowed myself, I turned right and followed the glass windows which extended through a range of shops selling books, perfumes, phones and stationery. Continuing past the brightly lit windows of the jewellers, with their glistening arrays of baubles, trinkets, rings, chains and watches, I turned right to where the mall opened into a large circular dome with fake palm trees rising out of huge pots full of pebbles, reaching for the sky through the glazed roof.

Here on display was the latest model Toyota car advertising the local agent, to the side of which was a patio-style garden setting and a coffee shop with wicker seats and marbled tables, where people sat chatting over coffee and passing the time of day.

In the distance, twin escalators moved in opposite directions, taking people to and from the first floor level where there was a restaurant with tables on a balcony. Here customers could look down onto the visitors dashing busily below.

Turning right, I followed the tiled floor through to the main central arcade, which opened into another larger, circular dome with a walkway crossing to the high street, and where the main seating area surrounded fountains and a water feature, the bottom of which was covered with coins. It has always fascinated me that people have this overwhelming desire to throw coins into water features, though I'm pleased that charities benefit from this frivolity.

The area was the hub of the shopping mall, bustling with activity as people criss-crossed from one mall to the other, pushing buggies or trolleys in and out of automatic, sliding doorways, swing doors and shop fronts. Some shops had competing music thumping out rhythms to drown the overall tannoy sound, which for me created a real strain on the ears when passing. Other shops had a more relaxed, subdued style of soothing sounds to lull customers into purchasing their goods.

Passing through to the far doors that automatically opened out onto the high street, I proceeded first to the bank and then to the chemist, a general store and the indoor market. I dawdled back towards the fountain where I had arranged to meet my husband, window-shopping on the way. We usually went our separate ways and did our own personal bits of shopping before meeting for a coffee around midday. We would then make arrangements either to look for items needing a shared decision or perhaps a critical eye together, or for an item of clothing or something we were not sure about, or planned to make tracks for the final supermarket shopping.

The mall cleaning ladies, with their trolley carts loaded with brushes, cloths and numerous other cleaning items, seemed to be continually sweeping up and cleaning in a continuous circuit, and the shopping mall was always spotlessly clean as a result. Passing one of these trolleys, I skirted the seats around the fountain where children were trailing their hands in the water. I stood and watched for a while as the rising and falling sprays continued to dance in front of me. Elderly ladies sat on the bench seats, resting weary legs, their shopping bags sprawled around their feet, as they chatted to their neighbours or just watched the world go by.

Mums sat feeding babies with bottles or mushy food from plastic containers. Toddlers were enjoying the freedom to stretch their legs running around the fountain pool. One toddler, in a hurry to escape a pursuing friend, almost ran into me and looked up laughing before turning to scream as his small playmate came closer. As he quickly dodged round me to continue his flight, I glanced at my watch and realised I had time to kill.

Looking around to see if there was any sign of my husband (even though I knew it was highly unlikely he would arrive early), I decided to browse for a little while in one of the corner shops. I walked through the entrance onto the thickly carpeted floor of a greetings card shop. Wall-to-wall shelving boasted an impressive array of cards, paper, boxes and trinkets, alongside ribbons, wrappings and balloons for every occasion and celebration you could think of.

Pausing to look at the humorous cards and picking out one or two that caught my eye, I smiled to myself and returned them to their slot. Funny how you could always find a card to suit a personal situation—but only after the event! It was always the way. A friend has a particularly awkward moment in a job and, months later, here is the ideal card that would have very aptly marked the occasion. Alas, the moment is past and lost. Someone finds they have passed an exam or test after they have told you all the things they thought they had done wrong, and here is a card, which just fits the category, but the humour will no longer fit and the moment is gone for ever.

Several assistants were scattered around the shop, fidgeting, tidying, patting, lifting cards out of racks, changing positions and putting them back behind other cards, always ready to volunteer help should it be needed or just keeping a watchful eye on customers. A quick glance at my watch told me I should be making my way to the arranged meeting place where my husband would be waiting. As I turned to leave, I came face-to-face with a sign blazoned across the top of a pile of boxes, which read: '2 for the price of one', and beneath it in small letters: 'buy one, get one free'.

My earlier light-hearted spirit was immediately dampened. As I approached the display, a feeling of despair, a flip of the stomach, and an overwhelming anger, began to rise in my chest. Looking at the boxes of glittering gold and silver cards, I really couldn't believe that anyone would be interested in this merchandise. It was the end of August for heaven's sake. Who in their right mind would consider buying a box of these cards? Obviously the shop staff thought someone would or they wouldn't have been put on display.

An elderly lady was standing nearby, also looking at the display, and she looked up at me and said, 'What month is it? August, I thought.'

'Funny, that's what I thought,' I replied, and giving one last look of disgust I turned and left, thinking better of the inclination to stick my foot out and topple the display as I passed to make my exit. The spell of the morning was broken. What had made me so angry and dampened my euphoric mood? The boxes on display contained Christmas cards!

# CHAPTER 1
## December

Since the end of October signs of Christmas had been gathering pace and all the shop windows were now highly decorated. Everywhere, items were adorned with tinsel and baubles, both tasteful and tacky, dangling amid displays ranging from clothes to food. The music had changed its tone from pop to carols, and Christmas songs, old and new, rang out. Coloured lights twinkled and flashed on trees of all shapes and sizes, now covered in fake snow or glitter. Streets were lit up with big, decorative, festive lights and streamers criss-crossed the walkways.

Every time you ran into a friend or neighbour during a shopping trip, the conversation revolved around what you had already purchased, what else you needed to buy, what you didn't have, and what you were still looking for. How far forward were your preparations? How were your plans going? It was all so exhausting and repetitive, the same ritual year in, year out. I would have preferred Christmas to appear and disappear all in the space of December, and even then, that would have been too long.

I tried to ignore it for as long as I could. The day that the first Christmas card landed on the doormat was the day I knew I could no longer delay. With dread, I made preparations to get the cards, make the lists, answer the letters, plan the visits to friends and family (which I considered to be an annual ritual), and think about what food to buy. It usually took two or three days to visit the friends and family we needed to see before Christmas, so arrangements had to be made about staying overnight somewhere whilst ensuring that our arrangements fitted in with everyone else's.

When that first card arrived, I always felt the panic rise at the thought that I would never get everything done in time. Christmas seemed to start far too early, yet still managed to rapidly rush in on me. However well organised I thought I was, everything would suddenly catch up with me so there was always a last minute rush and panic.

I sat at the dining room table, surrounded by boxes and packets of sparkling, seasonal cards of all types, from traditional and religious to humorous and children's, with just one or two odd cards left over from last year. There was also a pile of letters awaiting replies, some of which had arrived in last year's cards and others arriving throughout the year, as yet unanswered. In front of me lay an assortment of pens, paper, envelopes, stamps of various denominations, and airmail stickers, alongside the trusty address book and Christmas card list. This, of course, had been updated to include changes of address and, sadly, the deletions of friends and relatives no longer with us.

Unable to summon up the enthusiasm to get started, I sat looking into the garden. Blackbirds chased each other in and out of the heather, whilst a robin interrupted his meal on top of the bird table to watch them. Though the weather was overcast, the garden was rich with red and golden hues on the evergreen trees and shrubs, intentionally planted to display contrasting colour and interest all year round.

I began to think about how friends and relatives celebrated their Christmas and, in particular, the American style, which really appealed to me. There, the tree is usually brought in and put up on Christmas Eve, so that it creates a surprise and glorious spectacle on Christmas Day for the younger members of the family, whilst the older ones usually decorate it and place gifts below the spreading branches. This gives Christmas morning an extra magical feel and sense of fun. In the following twelve days the needles have little time to wilt or drop, remaining fresh and green until the tree is disposed of on Twelfth Night, when all the trimmings are lovingly packed away for another year.

My thoughts strayed to family and friends in warmer climes, such as Australia, Spain and various parts of America. Christmas must be a very different arrangement, with the hot sunshine and beach holiday atmosphere. Far more leisurely and with a completely different style and seasonal menu. I wondered how they coped with the chore (for that is my experience of it) of preparing for the Season of Goodwill.

It was then I thought, 'That's the whole point! Why do we call this the "Season of Goodwill"?' Surely there is no 'season' but three hundred and sixty-five days in every year when we should all be good, kind, loving and giving to each other, not just for a season or a period of a few days.

Although I was well aware of the Christian meaning of Christmas, my family was not religious. We had never been brought up to go to church so this aspect of the season was meaningless in our household. The only time family members attended church was for christenings, weddings or funerals (commonly referred to as 'hatched', 'matched' and 'despatched'). The only other visits to church for me had been on trips with the school years ago.

The more I wondered and reasoned, the more I questioned my intense loathing for Christmas. True, I didn't like the short, dreary days and the long, dark evenings of December, when everything seemed so drab and overcast, with a chill in the air and the prospect of worse to come. For a long time my doctor considered me to be a SAD case. He wasn't being rude, merely suggesting that I suffered from a condition known as 'Seasonal Affective Disorder'. To combat this at home there were bright lights in areas of the house where I spent a lot of time, but the dismal, grey days of winter still got me down. If the sun shone I would make the most of the opportunity to get out into the garden or go for a walk. Even so, I intensely disliked this time of year. The bare trees and empty fields, sheep nosing about in the soil hoping in vain for a tasty green shoot to munch, just made it seem all the more awful, a horrid time of year.

Of course, there were other, much deeper reasons for how I felt about Christmas that went much further back in time. As I sat reflecting, my mind drifted back to childhood days and Christmases of long ago. When we were children, my father had always drummed into my brother and me that you got nothing in this life unless you worked for it. We didn't get pocket money handouts. Every penny had to be deserved. Shopping, gardening, cleaning the car, running errands, helping around the house—we earned our pocket money.

From the time I was considered old enough, I had been getting up at six o'clock every morning to cover a paper round. In that time I chopped and changed to different rounds and became the only person in the shop who knew them all. There were twenty of us hired by the newsagent, mostly boys of course, but there were a couple of elderly gentlemen subsidising their pensions, three women who needed extra income to help pay the bills, and myself and one other girl. If the papers were late arriving at the newsagents it made the children late with their rounds, so I made sure that I knew how to gather up my own papers, magazines and journals and write my own round up. By the time I was fourteen, the round I covered involved a five-mile cycle route on the outskirts of town, the wages from which gave me some freedom and independence.

This meant that, from an early age, I learned to budget well and never skimped on presents. When Christmas arrived, I was able to buy some nice presents for friends and family, often the little extras I bought costing more than the main gifts. A lot of thought went into my purchases and I always got more pleasure from the giving than the receiving of presents.

My own presents were very often just opened and put aside, and it wouldn't have worried me if I'd not received any presents at all, or even been given just one gift. I had very simple tastes and didn't crave expensive toys or personal items. I had no real interest in clothes as a youngster as mine were not of my own choosing and selected mainly for school, with just one or two items for best purchased by my mother (with no consideration as to what I may like or dislike!).

On reflection then, it was not money or the cost that worried me. I just longed to get away from it all, even ignore it altogether. Let those who wished to celebrate do so, but I just wanted to be somewhere far away where Christmas was not celebrated, and I could be left alone. I would have been happy and content to buy presents for everyone, tell them not to bother spending money on me, just to enjoy the season and celebrations while my husband and I would go off somewhere where Christmas had never been heard of. I just couldn't wait for it to all be over and done with, forgotten for another year, so that life could get back to normal and sanity would again prevail.

As I pondered on Christmases past, a strange sadness came over me. I seemed to be watching the whole of my life unfold, as if on a film being played back to me. The answers were all there, somewhere in the past, waiting to be unfolded, offering insight and reasons as to why I would want Christmas postponed, and even hope that it would never arrive. I seemed to be moving through a chasm, to a place in time gone by. Memories were awakening, feelings being stirred, vivid pictures quickly began taking shape …

# CHAPTER 2
## The Learning Curve

On reflection I suppose I did love my father, in a strangely ambivalent sort of way, but the mental and physical scars of our relationship are with me to this day.

When he was in a good humour, he was fun to be with, playing with my brother and me, and taking us swimming. But, if we upset him or stepped out of line we would be thrashed. Depending upon the severity of our behaviour, we would suffer either his large, heavy hands across our legs, a slipper across the backside or a leather strap, which left great red weals across our buttocks.

I was about ten or eleven years old when, for speaking out of turn one time at the dinner table, I was hit with what should have been the flat of the blade of my father's knife. I now have a scar on my left arm where he drew blood. He always had the sharpest knife, a memento from his army days.

My brother and I were ruled with a rod of iron. I can still hear the very words Mother used to threaten us whenever we were in trouble: 'Wait till your father comes home.' We would then go to our room and, with mounting dread, await his arrival home from work and the ensuing consequences following Mother's relaying of the offending event to him. We quickly learned not to relate at home those events at school which had earned us a ruler across the knuckles or a caning, since we would get another hiding from our parents.

I can still picture Father dressed in his paint-spattered overalls, a paint can in one hand and a brush in the other, going up and down ladders. He would always whistle while he worked and occasionally his pleasant voice would break into song. He loved his job.

As a very professional worker and good at what he did, Father was employed by a number of wealthy people, whose wives he considered to be as fair game as any to coax into bed. According to him, professional men's wives couldn't resist 'a bit of rough' on the side. He bragged that it added excitement to their dull and boring lives that were otherwise full of coffee mornings and charity work. So, in between hanging expensive wallpapers, he spent quite a lot of time between silk sheets. 'If they're big enough, they're old enough, and anything from fourteen to eighty years old is fair game,' was his philosophy.

Hypocritically, this only applied to himself and certainly not to his daughter, since any male seen showing any interest in me resulted in them being warned off, even before reaching the holding hands stage in some cases! I was a pretty, blonde-haired, blue-eyed child and was always daddy's little girl. The trouble was, I wasn't allowed to grow up and be anyone else's girl. I wasn't allowed the freedom many of my friends enjoyed. I wasn't overly worried about not attending dances or going to the youth club, as I needed to get up early for my paper round anyway, so it was something I learned to accept. When my friends had parties I was only allowed to go if it was to be an all-girl affair and with adult supervision. I had to wear my best school uniform and regulation lace-up brogues. I just felt so frumpy and old-fashioned, totally embarrassed in front of my friends who now wore bras and stockings, casual slip-on shoes and feminine clothes, that I would borrow clothes from friends and change when I arrived. Later on, when I had my own money, I was able to buy the clothes and shoes that I wanted. They didn't always meet with my parents' approval so I would leave home in my ordinary clothes, take my 'best outfits' in a bag and change when I arrived at the party or wherever it was I was going.

Looking back over the years, I remember women drifting in and out of our lives. There were many arguments between my parents over women, and we even had one turn up on our doorstep suggesting Mother should leave my father! It was when I was about nine years old. Mother had either heard rumours or started to suspect that Father was being unfaithful. What aroused the suspicion to begin with, I don't know, but one night I was woken from sleep by a knock at the front door. On answering it, Mother was confronted by a woman who asked if she could come in and speak to her on a 'private matter'. Mother only allowed her into the hall and asked what she wanted, having told her to keep her voice down as 'the children are asleep'. From what I could overhear, it seemed that the woman had been seeing my father and wanted my mother to consider divorcing him. The two women had, up until then, been talking in whispers but, at this pronouncement, my mother told the woman in no uncertain terms to get out and leave us, and my father, alone. Whether Mother believed what she told the woman next, I don't know, but it came as a shock to me. She said that my father had been involved with other women as far back as she could remember, and that she (the woman) was just another notch on the bedpost, and probably wouldn't be the last. Mother added that my father would soon tire of her and that he would return to his family as he had always done.

I remember my mother weeping afterwards. I tried to go back to sleep but could only cry in fear of the inevitable forthcoming arguments. I was also terrified that perhaps she was wrong and that my father would desert us, and I worried about what would happen to us all. When the rows and fights about this particular woman actually took place, I can't remember, it all seems too vague now, but the affair was discontinued, my mother forgave my father once again, and things got back to 'normal'. This meant that Mother and Father were again lovey-dovey towards each other, touching, laughing, play-fighting, kissing and cuddling, at any time, regardless of whether we were around or not.

However, one Sunday afternoon my brother and I went for a walk with my mother around the village. She obviously knew that a certain woman was visiting relatives, and she just wanted to get something out of her system. We were on a part of the housing estate that we didn't normally visit, and, passing a garden where there were several people standing around talking, we saw a young woman holding a tiny child in her arms. The woman happened to turn and point to the sky, to show the child a plane, and caught sight of us as she did so. She blushed deeply and turned away. The little girl in her arms had blonde curly hair and was the image of myself at her age. I could only guess that the woman was the same one who made the clandestine visit to my mother, and that the child was the fruit of the affair.

This was the first time I really became aware of Father's attraction for women. As time went on, it became obvious that he had an insatiable appetite for sex. Father had a reputation for being a 'Jack the Lad' and, even though he was married to my mother, he still wanted to run with the fox and hunt with the hounds. He made a pretty good attempt at doing both. My father was a very vain man. Whilst in the army he had the same regulation short back and sides as every other soldier, but once back on civvy street he went through phases, from having a quiff slicked back with Brylcreem and eased into a wave, to a crew cut which made him appear hard. He would stand in front of a mirror for quite a while, being very fussy over his appearance.

There was an occasion when Mother had gone into hospital for an operation on varicose veins. A friend who lived only five minutes walk away came in to help out. My father and her husband, a local policeman, were good friends and they all often went out together as a foursome. It just so happened that Thursday was market day in the town and my grandmother had called in one lunchtime, breaking her bus journey into town, to see that everything was alright. She opened the passage door leading to the back door and, on glancing through the side window, saw my father and Mother's friend hurriedly straightening their clothes and hair. Grandmother knocked on the door and, without waiting, opened it and walked in. Her spluttering, embarrassed son-in-law managed to mutter, 'Hello, I didn't expect to see you here today,' to which my grandmother replied, 'Obviously not!' The shocked and embarrassed best friend's wife made her excuses and a very hasty exit, leaving my father to put things straight. My grandmother had wanted to know how my mother was and he could do nothing short of running her to the hospital for a visit as he returned to work.

Over time, Mother was to become a brilliant detective, able to spot not only the obvious signs—make-up and lipstick on his shirts, perfume and hairs on his jackets, even finding a pair of knickers in the pocket of his overcoat—but also other subtle indications. Father's behaviour would give him away, he had a certain way of strutting, and the way he dressed too. His character also changed when there was another woman in his life.

Confronting him on numerous occasions Mother would say, 'To be a good liar you have to have a brilliant memory, and when you've been drinking your memory fails you.' He would tell her she was paranoid, had a vivid imagination and was distrusting. They would argue and fight, and mother would burst into tears, sometimes locking herself in the bedroom so Father ended up sleeping on the sofa. There were other times when he would force the bedroom door open, and proceed to beat and rape her. It was nothing for me to come home from school or shopping to find her on her hands and knees, polishing out her frustration on a large piece of furniture, crying and talking to herself. She never allowed my father to see her this way though, and I tried not to let her know that I'd seen or heard anything.

When things had been happy between them my parents got on very well together, and, during the early years of their marriage, had a highly active sex life. Father had an insatiable sexual appetite and Mother was always ready to oblige him. They were very loving and passionate towards each other and not afraid to show it. Whether they were sexually active before they married, I don't know, but I do know that my father had become sexually active as a lad, when he was staying in Somerset. He was very forward and no doubt needed little encouragement when invited to get help with lessons from a young schoolteacher. As well as any academic help, she also gave my father sexual coaching, thereby developing his potential—as an ardent lover!

However, the passion of the early years vanished and was overtaken by sex and lust, certainly on my father's part. He would expect my mother to have sex at the drop of a hat, any time of the night or day, very often coming home for lunch for that reason alone. The problem was, he didn't always work locally and his insatiable appetite meant he needed sex and more sex, so he continued to look elsewhere for it at every opportunity.

Father caused my mother to suffer no end of agonising situations and utter humiliation on several occasions. He flirted in front of her and tried to encourage her to do the same, in order to justify his own actions. He would belittle her in company, whether they were out together socially or at home with friends, and it wouldn't be unusual, on an evening out together, for Mother to arrive home alone. I remember on one occasion Mother returning home in a terrible temper after it was suggested to her they attend a wife-swapping evening. She had seen all the keys on the table in the middle of the room, but didn't realise this was the lottery. The keys picked up from the table by an individual would identify who was to be their bed partner for the rest of the evening. Mother tried to laugh it off, until she realised that everyone else was serious. She went hysterical, and left.

Father's sexual appetite knew no bounds, extending even to his own daughter. As children, my brother and I would climb into bed with our parents at the weekends. My mother was always the first to get up since she complained that we were always wriggling and fidgeting. She probably dreaded us poking our heads round the door and creeping in. Once Mother was up my brother was not far behind, and that left me cuddled up snugly with my father. Soon, he started to rub my nipples and tell me I had beautiful little rosebuds. I used to think it was funny and giggle.

Usually, when I got up, he would kiss me and I would go back to my bedroom and get dressed. However, on one occasion, having got into my parents' bed and had the usual cuddle, my father began to run his hand up my leg. He attempted to fondle my 'pussy', as he called it. I became very frightened, slapped his hand away, and jumped out of bed. I was very wary of my father for a long time after this incident, and it was never mentioned. Needless to say, I never got into bed with my parents again, always excusing myself by insisting I was now getting too big and grown up for Sunday morning cuddles.

During my final two senior school years, I would often go along at weekends and during holidays to where my father was working, and strip large rooms of wallpaper to earn some extra pocket money, while my father was supposedly out purchasing materials for the job in hand. It never occurred to me until much later that, while I was doing his work for him, he was spending time somewhere else with his latest conquest. I don't know why I never questioned the rumours. Perhaps I was naïve, or stupid, or simply wanted to shut out the truth. Sometimes his workmates would whisper about him, 'If they're big enough, they're old enough. That's all the guv'nor cares.'

Father was referred to either as 'the guv'nor' or 'guv' by the young apprentice lads who came along to help out and gain work experience. I often wondered what sort of experience these lads got. They would sometimes discuss their conquests in front of me (how much of it was true was anyone's guess). I felt sick just listening to them so I did my best to ignore them. Their behaviour led me to believe that men were all the same. As I got older, the language got worse, the obscenities more obscene. Perhaps they were just less careful in front of me now, or maybe they were trying to impress me! It never occurred to me they might be challenging me. Knowing that I couldn't help but hear every word, the discussions got louder as their excitement grew in the retelling of their latest antics, parading like cocks going into battle, and laughing.

Eventually, I became so uncomfortable working with the apprentices, feeling embarrassed when they tried to include me in their conversations, that I was reluctant to help out on any more jobs. They would flirt with me and use expressions I didn't understand, but these lads knew better than to ask me out (Father was very strict about where I went and who I kept company with). It was quite a few years before I became aware that some of the things they had said to me were so crude I was quite happy that I hadn't understood them. Had Father known about what was happening at work when he was not there I was sure then that he would have been none too pleased. Or would he? Could there have been an ulterior motive in allowing me to work there, that I would find out about life and what went on in the outside world from people he knew or over whom he had some influence and control?

He certainly had a way with women, with the gift of the gab and that 'come hither' look, and the trouble was the women all seemed to fall for it! A womaniser who wasn't fussy about age, looks, colour, race or creed, Father viewed any woman wearing a skirt who responded to wolf whistles and flattery as 'fair game'.

I came to learn it was common knowledge that Father had been with any number of women, had had a child with at least one and also attended a VD clinic. I always tried to block the knowledge out, like it was all a bad dream. If I didn't think about it I could pretend nothing happened or it didn't matter, or even that it wouldn't happen again. But, of course, it always did, even at Christmas.

# CHAPTER 3
## My Retreat

Whether my mother ever really loved me is doubtful, she certainly rarely showed any sign of affection towards me. Perhaps that's why my brother and I never got on from the time he was born. I suppose it was partly jealousy since he got all the attention and I didn't, but I also hated the crying, the screaming, the nappy changing, feeding and so on. Whenever people asked me what I thought of my little brother I would usually tell them I hated him or that I thought he was a nuisance. As we grew up, we grew as far apart as it was possible to get, until I reached the point where I loathed him, and I'm sure the feeling was mutual.

In the same way I was 'daddy's little girl', my brother was always Mother's favourite, and, somehow, he always seemed completely oblivious of the relationship problems between my parents. As the older child, I was always protective of him and defended him when he was in trouble outside, yet he would torment me and get me into trouble. Perhaps it was because I was Father's favourite, and Father only ever scorned him from an early age, often telling him how stupid and thick he was, and never giving him any encouragement. As Mother's favourite, my brother always chose to ignore the way I was treated by her and would never listen to my concerns about how she acted towards me.

It's possible my mother drove my father into the arms of other women. She was cold, calculating, and filled with hate and jealousy for everyone. As a child she had always been jealous of her younger sister, whom she considered to be spoiled and who was given much more freedom than she was. Jealous of her sister's boyfriend, and of the gifts he bought her, Mother actually tore a necklace from her sister's throat in a fit of rage just because it was a present from him.

Mother was obsessed with having her own private nest egg and so she would always be working and cleaning, in order to save money. She built barriers that were hard to penetrate so I found it very difficult to talk to her about anything and, by the time she and my father divorced, she had become hard and bitter.

Not so my grandmother, the biggest influence in my life. A lovely, short, round, fat, cheerful lady, she was a wonderful person who was always happy, and always willing to listen and advise without ever chastising or interfering. Nan was the one who taught me all the things that make me who I am and, even now, when I picture her in the garden, I can hear her calling my name, as if she were still here watching over me.

During my young childhood, my grandparents lived in a large council house in a lovely Hertfordshire village called Hatfield Heath, which was within walking or biking distance from us. Despite its size, the house always seemed warm and welcoming. I remember there was a big mangle with heavy rubber rollers which stood in the corner of the scullery, alongside the washtub and wooden wash dolly. Mondays were always washdays, and the extensive washing line running alongside the garden path would be used from end to end, unless of course it was raining, when the pulley and airing horse would come to the rescue.

Nan had lots of patience and would sit with me for hours, teaching me to knit, do needlework and even make paper flowers from coloured tissue paper. If things went wrong she would help me undo or unravel things and then show me all over again how to do it right. I also learned to cook using her good, basic, old-fashioned methods, and how to do gardening. In my grandparents house there were always flowers, which Nan grew herself. My grandfather, a labourer who dug roads and suchlike for a living, grew all his own vegetables, fruits and salad in the large garden. Nan had her own section where she grew herbs, and in the borders she put flowers and shrubs. When I was old enough to get on a bus by myself, I would go to my nan's house on a Friday evening and stay over until as late as possible on the Sunday, before having to go home. I loved the warmth and joy of sleeping on an ancient feather bed, the mattress of which would wrap itself around me as I snuggled into it and make me feel as though I was being cuddled.

Whenever my parents had a big row, or they were holding one of their week-long silences, I just couldn't wait to get to my nan's house, away from the dreadful atmosphere. When they weren't arguing over other women, there were heated arguments arising from other things. For example, my parents would attend whist drives and, unfortunately, Mother was not a very good player. Father could remember every card laid, knew exactly what cards Mother held in her hand, and would spend the next two days criticising her game and telling her what a useless partner she was. The atmosphere at home during these times was dreadful. It affected my schoolwork and, when at home, I would often sit in the bedroom to keep out of the way. And, not only did I have to contend with my parents' behaviour, there was also my brother to worry about. He would torment me, tease me and was generally really hateful. I couldn't abide him, or his friends.

The atmosphere at my grandparents' house was far more harmonious than home and I just loved to be with them. It was Nan with whom I shared my joys and sorrows. I could tell her anything and everything, and never be judged. Offering advice and a shoulder to cry on when things went wrong, she was a real treasure. I had lots of boyfriends during my teenage years and I introduced them all to my nan for her approval and opinion long before they were ever to meet my parents, if at all.

And so, it was to my nan that I turned for help and advice when I found myself unmarried and pregnant, and it was her guidance that was to stand me in good stead for the things to come. Her own married life hadn't got off to a good start. My great-grandmother, a Queen Victoria double, was well set in Victorian ways, so, when my nan became pregnant at the age of nineteen, a 'shotgun wedding' was arranged, with all the parents making sure that the knot was well and truly tied long before any scandal could develop.

I don't know what reaction my grandmother had from her parents, but the day I had to admit to my mother that I was pregnant, I received mouthfuls of verbal abuse, followed by a good beating from my father. Mother had told me that I was pregnant before I had even been diagnosed. I said that she was just being spiteful, whilst at the same time praying that she was wrong and hoping for a miscarriage if she was right. A week before I was due to marry the father of my child, I did something or other to offend and was threatened with, 'While you live under our roof you abide by our rules. You are not too old for a good hiding.' I was twenty years and six months old, and three months pregnant!

My own parents, in particular my father, wanted me to have a big white wedding. I refused and we settled on a registry office affair. He just wanted to be able to show friends and family that I was getting a good 'send off', and so a large reception at a local restaurant was organised, attended by a hundred guests, followed by an evening dance to which an additional fifty friends were invited.

By this time in my life I was only too pleased to be leaving home, to get away from a father whom I considered to be even more of a hypocrite following the events which filled me with fear, grief and loathing, when I was just fifteen years old.

# CHAPTER 4
## The Early Years

Father was the youngest of nine children from East Ham in the East End of London. With four brothers and four sisters, he was a real boisterous, cocky, Cockney kid who was always in a bit of bother. The trouble was, he was also cheeky and likeable.

When war was first declared my father had been sent to Somerset with hundreds of other children from London but, when nothing seemed to be happening and things remained quiet, families wanted their children back and so they returned home. During the Blitz, however, it was decided to quickly despatch children to villages and the countryside surrounding London thirty miles away, far enough away to feel safe and be out of the direct line of fire.

Father was taken to the village of Hatfield Heath where, as he grew older, he became a bit of a Jack the Lad, with a swagger about him that made him popular with the girls in the village. He joined in the village cricket and football games, as well as the fights and brawls that often occurred between the locals and the Londoners. Later, he grew into a dashing, good-looking, tall, dark, stocky man with blue eyes and a cheeky grin. The local village boys felt they had been invaded by the enemy, and village life was never to be the same again.

Mother, on the other hand, was the middle of three children, with an older brother and a younger sister. They had been born, and still lived, in a tiny village on the Essex/Hertfordshire border, where everyone knew everyone else. She had a slim build and was of medium height, very pretty with lovely long mid-brown hair, which she used to twist in rags to give it gentle waves or ringlets. With her hazel eyes and a shy little-girl-lost look, Mother became a target for the London lad who swept her off her feet. Shy she certainly wasn't, and was easily able to look after herself, having a brother with whom she often fought and a sister who allowed herself to be bossed and bullied.

Suddenly, the horizons for all the local kids were broadened and, although not everyone welcomed the intrusion of these London children with open arms, they certainly livened up the quiet village life. Lots of hearts were broken along the way, with old boyfriends and girlfriends loosing out to the newly arrived talent and there was heated rivalry amongst them all.

When Father caught my mother's eye, this resulted in trouble between her and her childhood sweetheart. She had been courting a local boy for years. They had known each other since they had been babes in arms, gone to school together, played together and, until war broke out and lives had been thrown into complete disarray by these marauding London kids, it had been taken for granted that they would eventually marry.

At the end of the war my father was called up to do his National Service. Never afraid of work and always out to earn some extra money, he would turn his hand to anything. He helped to deliver coal and also worked with a local joiner and decorator, picking up lots of experience that was to stand him in good stead for the future.

Father managed to work his way up to become a corporal in the army and was also trained while in the services to take an active interest in sport, boxing being a particular favourite. For part of his service time in the army he was posted to Italy and thoroughly enjoyed the experience, never having been abroad before.

Of the American GIs it was always said they were 'overpaid, over-sexed and over here'. It is quite possible that the Italians thought the same about the British troops after the war. It seemed that my father managed to earn himself quite a reputation with his unit for being able to attract plenty of Italian women. He was known for being hard working and hard loving.

Meanwhile, Mother was also working hard, in a factory. Having left the village school at fourteen years of age, and not a very good scholar, she became a scullery maid in a local businessman's large country house. She was one of a large number of staff employed to run the house and the estate. Most of the permanent service staff—the housekeeper, cook, butler and the children's governess—all lived in, but the chambermaid, chauffeur, gardeners and my mother went home.

They all worked very long hours, six days a week, scrubbing floors and whitening steps, blacking grates, treating the kitchen floor with red cardinal polish, and cleaning brass and silver, week in, week out. Mother was just one of several hired help who were at the family's beck and call. The children had no respect for the servants whatever their status and would very often deliberately tread muddy boots on the newly whitened steps, trail dirt across the clean floors so that they had to be cleaned a second time from buckets of water and rung out floor-cloths, on hands and knees.

The onset of war gave my mother a chance to move away from the life of servitude. A local factory began offering well-paid assembly work to anyone who wanted it, making parts for the Spitfire aeroplanes. Recognising a good opportunity when she saw it, my mother applied and was accepted. This was a big move up the ladder for my mother and other local girls and boys, expanding their outlook on life, earning higher wages, working shift work and overtime, and also widening their social circles. My mother spent her leisure time waiting for my father to come home on leave, when he would spend time back in the village.

At home on leave in 1946, he married my mother in the village church. I arrived nine months later, a few months before my father was demobbed. Up to this time my mother had lived in the family home. When my father came home for good they moved into a tiny tar-washed, clapboard cottage with a slated roof situated in an isolated area of the countryside, with farm workers for neighbours on one side and an elderly widow on the other. The cottages were owned and rented out by a farmer whose own property was half a mile down the lane. The only other neighbour lived hermit-like in a pretty cottage covered in ivy with rambling roses over the porch, situated half-way between the farm and our cottage. A large thatched house stood in an orchard and could be seen across the fields about half a mile away (as the crow flies) on a twisting lane leading to the next village. There were a few more houses in a hamlet at the end of the lane that lay in a dip out of sight of the cottages.

The cottages shared a yard, in the middle of which was a water pump, the overflow running into the ditch alongside it and beyond the primroses and violets growing under the hazel and hawthorn hedge. On the far side of the yard Father built a shed in which to store tools, paints, ladders, bicycles and, later on, Father's moped. So that space was not taken up from the yard and the shed was out of the way, it was balanced on large timbers resting on each bank of a stream, which then ran underneath it. This shed was also used as a workshop and lots of useful items were made as Father's carpentry and joinery skills were put into practice.

The yard was part of a footpath and bridleway used by horse-riders, farm-workers and walkers, as a shortcut across the fields to another hamlet. Just outside the yard, on the side of the road, was a large pond where we would collect frogspawn and tadpoles. In the lane opposite there was a magnificent oak tree and, a little further on, a very large elm. There were ditches running alongside the hedgerows, full of primroses and violets in the spring. Every year bluebells carpeted the ground of several small copses, and larger woods lay within walking distance.

The cottage itself was warm and cosy. A tiny two-up, two-down, it was very primitive and there were no modern facilities. The door from the shared yard opened straight into the kitchen where stairs went up on the left and the long, bleach-scrubbed bench table went along the whole of the front wall beneath the window. My mother did everything on this table, from washing and ironing to food preparation. It was scrubbed regularly and the wooden grain was uneven. On the opposite side of the room was a dresser holding every item of crockery, glass and kitchenware my parents possessed, and where food was stored. A cupboard under the stairs was used for keeping coats and shoes hidden from view as well as cans and jars of food. It was also the place where my father's poaching coat hung, covering the shotgun he took with him when he went shooting.

We often had pheasant, rabbit, hare and pigeon on the table, as did many other people who lived in the countryside. There was no cooker during the early years and everything was cooked in one large pot on a primus stove. Water was boiled for washing, laundry and cleaning in a large covered bucket, and baking was done in the range at the side of the fire in the main room. My mother learned to cook food in a pressure cooker during this time but, after a while, a cooker fuelled by bottles of Calor gas was bought. Once Calor gas was piped in, gas lamps were fitted downstairs to replace candles and oil lamps, though these were still used in the bedrooms. The gas lamps, which hissed and spluttered, had fragile mantles that were expensive to replace and disintegrated when they expired.

Also purchased was a copper in which to boil the laundry and, using water heated in it, baths were taken in front of the fire in a galvanised tin bath which was usually hung on the inside of the kitchen door.

Opposite the kitchen door, between the cupboard under the stairs and the dresser, another door opened into a square room with a pretty, floral-patterned three-piece suite and an enormous fireplace that took up most of the available space. Either side of the wide, bare-bricked chimney-breast were shelves for books and ornaments. A coal scuttle and log basket sat on either side of the hearth with handmade rag scatter-rugs carpeting the floor. The black-leaded range and the polished copper hearth fender both gleamed and the companion set hung on a wrought iron stand nearby. I get a warm feeling when I remember how we used to sit around the fire in this room toasting crumpets, the toasting fork against the hot coals, seeming to take for ever to brown. It was so cosy.

When the hearth was empty and the fire unmade, the sky could be viewed through the top of the chimney. The mantelshelf was made of a thick oak beam on which photos and brass pots were displayed, and where letters and papers in a rack stood above horse brasses hanging down the side. Hanging on a chain from a hook fixed into a beam above the mantelshelf was a mirror. The ceilings were very low with dark, gnarled and knotted wooden beams at regular intervals. The internal doors were also low and both my parents had to remember to duck their heads in and out of the rooms. All the doors had heavy, woollen, khaki blankets hanging over them from a pole on curtain rings. These were drawn together in the winter to prevent draughts and tied back in the summer to one side.

The cottage had two bedrooms. I shared the one to the right at the top of the stairs with my brother. It had no door and there was a small rail to prevent falling into the stairwell. Simply furnished, there was a cot for him, a small single bed for me, and a chest of drawers that served us both. Our toys were kept in a box stored under the top end of the bed and we each had a chamber pot at the bottom end. If I had been naughty and got sent to this room, I could sit on my bed and look across the fields, trying to see if anything was moving, or counting how many rabbits or other interesting things I could see. That way, punishment seemed fairly enjoyable.

A door opposite the top of the stairs led into the large bedroom containing a large narrowing chimney-breast rising up the middle, a double bed, a dressing table with three angled mirrors against the window, and a wardrobe. Like all children, I used to love to get into my parents' bed and snuggle between them for a cuddle.

The bedroom windows were small with several squared panes of glass and each had pretty floral curtains. Mother was fairly clever with her hands and made lots of items for the cottage herself. Curtains and cushion covers were made from remnants of material, clothes picked up at rummage sales were unpicked or altered, rugs and mats made from rags torn into strips and worked into a sack backing cloth. Most of our jumpers, cardigans, vests, socks, gloves, hats and scarves were all hand knitted, and any good quality woollen items found in sales were often unravelled, skeined, washed and then re-knitted.

Outside the cottage was a long, narrow garden planted with rows of vegetables and flowers, a result of the 'dig for victory' campaign in the war years. With rationing books still in use, most families grew their own vegetables. The garden was reached through a door on the far side of the living room, which opened onto a path made of ashes and cinders. This path led to the privy, a quaint, tiny, wooden shed, against which were stacked piles of ready cut logs, together with other pieces of wood and branches waiting to be sawn.

Once inside, there was just enough room to turn around in and it was dark, the only available light squeezing through the gap at the top of the door. Neat squares of newspaper hung on a hook at the side and a square box with folded toilet paper sheets sat on the seat. On a hook on the door hung a dried bunch of herbs to sweeten the offensive air. The door held a lift-up latch but no lock so humming (or, in my father's case, whistling) became a necessary pastime, along with the swinging of feet against the removable wooden panel fitted between the seat and floor, to ward against the embarrassment of being caught with your pants around your ankles!

With just a seat with a hole in, the privy seemed dark and forbidding, particularly to a small child, and was cold, draughty and uncomfortable. This was not a place one would want to hang around in for long and, for small children, held the additional fear of falling into the hole. Sitting alone on the seat, the imagination would run wild, conjuring up creepy, crawly, slimy images of things just waiting for tasty morsels to drop into open mouths. During the summer months the smell was pretty high and flies would swarm around—a veritable feast for the many spiders waiting in their webs, who seemed to get bigger at every visit, with great, fat, round bodies and long, spindly legs.

When the paper was high enough to tickle your bum it was clearly time for the privy to be emptied. So, every few weeks a deep pit was dug in a clear patch somewhere in the garden and the privy bucket emptied and the hole filled in. This was not a particularly thankful task, but worthwhile since the plants always flourished well. It was my father's job to empty the bucket and the smell from the upended bucket was appalling. The contents would slide out in a wet, sludgy mass and plop in the bottom of the hole. Stinking and pungent, the aroma would hang in the air for a long while, whilst my father would joke in his Cockney accent, 'Cor, that's a lovely drop o' stuff. The plants'll enjoy that, that'll make 'em grow.' After being emptied, the privy and the bucket were then cleaned and disinfected, the seat scrubbed and bleached. The walls were brushed clean of cobwebs and the clean smell was sweet and refreshing, though it didn't last for long.

In the winter the emptying of the bucket had to be timed to fit in with the weather since once the ground had frozen it was impossible to dig in the garden. As well as our own private sustenance, the garden was spread with farmyard manure once a year, dug in to 'enrich the soil'. Plants obviously had disgusting habits and yet there were always flowers in the house, either from the garden or the hedgerow, and all year round we had fresh vegetables from the garden.

I have fond memories of this simple cottage. The sun always seemed to shine and it is remembered as a happy place. There I learned to ride a bicycle, my mother was always cheerful, laughing and singing, and it was where my brother was born. We used to watch the huntsmen in their brightly coloured coats and shiny boots ride across the fields to the sound of the horn, the hounds baying in tow. Thankfully, I don't ever remember seeing them in pursuit of a fox.

When I was old enough to go to school, I joined the crocodile walk. The young boy from the farm collected two children from a house down a farm track before collecting me, and we all went to the end of the lane and collected four children from the house there, and, in passing, the two children from the thatched house in the orchard. We then crocodiled on to school, which was a three-mile walk each way mornings and evenings. As the older children moved on to senior school, the younger ones would join us to continue the process, so there were always about ten of us walking together by the time we reached the school gate.

On reflection, this was a time in my life remembered with warmth and affection. We used to play at the farm during the holidays and went out on the tractors and trailers during the harvesting. The farm had a lovely big tabby cat, which earned its keep by keeping control of the numbers of rats and mice around the place. There was also a lovely collie dog, which was kept in the barn, a working dog, both with the sheep and cattle, as well as being a good guard dog.

During the season, Mother would take us potato picking and pea picking, and we would enjoy a picnic lunch in the fields with all the other women and children and the farm workers. Several travellers and gypsies used to work on the farms during this time, and they all dressed the same. The women had cut sacks tied around their waists, the bottom of which they gathered in one hand whilst throwing potatoes or peas in with the other, and their heads were covered with a scarf tied up in turban style. It was tiring and back-breaking work and everyone was exhausted at the end of the day but it was well paid and didn't last for long, so it was worth doing. Once the fields were finished the field workers were allowed to go gleaning and this would be a worthwhile perk.

We would walk for miles across the fields and to the bluebell woods and would return with arms full of flowers. We used to pick kingcups in the marshland at the side of the meadow, and paddle in the stream or play Pooh-sticks under the bridge. The bridge was a short distance from a fork in the road and we would wait at the bridge sometimes so that we could get a ride on the lorry dropping off the workmen, which occasionally brought our father home. This was very exciting for us as the only other transport we ever travelled in, apart from the farm trailers, was a very rare bus or coach.

These early years were probably responsible for developing my love of country life, and the appreciation of nature and the natural environment that is important to me today. I learned the names of all the wild flowers and trees, and loved all the wildlife. We knew what it was like to be cut off during the winter and have to wait for the snow plough to come from the farm to clear the snow when the lane disappeared under four feet drifts. It was like a winter wonderland when the landscape was all one level with just the hedgerows poking out to show where the road should be. Living in the middle of fields, we would have to go into the main village by bicycle to catch a bus into town. Sometimes, we would cycle six miles to my grandparents' house, with my brother strapped into a child seat behind the saddle on Mother's bike. One thing we never had to worry about was traffic. We were lucky if we saw a car and the only traffic apart from the farm machinery was either service vehicles or lorries going to the farm.

I was about seven years old when my parents were offered the chance to move to a nearby village and into a new council house that contained all the modern advantages of piped water, electricity and a real bathroom. This was a big move for us, a chance to move up in the world. Unfortunately, there was a downside. We had already experienced one incident involving my father and another woman when, for a short time, a friend of my mother's lived in a caravan parked in a field adjacent to our garden. The friend had married and was waiting for council accommodation. Following a request from my father, the couple obtained permission from the farm owner to park on the field and use the pump belonging to the cottages. My father and the friend's husband would be collected for work by lorry each day, and my mother would visit the friend regularly.

After living in the caravan for some time, a rift developed between my mother and her friend, so she stopped visiting. The couple were eventually offered a council house in a nearby village and the friendship ended completely. Although I was not old enough to understand the reason for the broken friendship, I knew that it involved my father being caught in some compromising position with the friend when Mother just happened to visit unexpectedly.

Unfortunately, had we but known it, this was merely a forerunner for events to come. In moving to the new council estate, my father not only found his feet and made lots of new friends but also found the local pubs and loose women. Things were never to be the same again.

# CHAPTER 5
## The Visit

The new house never felt warm or cosy like the cottage had. It was big, cold and draughty, and never seemed really friendly or inviting when you came in the front door. The house had neither atmosphere nor character, and was just one in a row of very ordinary plain-looking brick-built houses. Apart from the number on the door, there was nothing to distinguish it from any other house in that road.

It was a really weird design too, with a front door and a door referred to as the 'back' door, side-by-side for convenience or access according to the designers at the council offices. Although the dustbin could be hidden behind a low wall and kept at the front of the house for easy collection, there was no access to the back garden except through the house. This meant that the coal and anything required for gardening had to be manoeuvred through the integral store room and kitchen to get to the door leading into the garden, also called the back door, just to cause confusion.

The 'side' door at the front of the house opened into a storeroom that could be used as an indoor shed for bikes and tools, and from which a door led into the kitchen. This was a bright, spacious room with a fairly high, long, narrow window that was difficult to reach, situated above the sink and draining board, either side of which were long work surfaces with cupboards underneath. The biggest asset the kitchen had was the enormous walk-in larder, with its four-inch thick cold concrete shelf for keeping items cool, and several wooden shelves reaching to the ceiling. The cooker was a modern piped gas type, which was on tap and only ran out of gas when someone forgot to put money in the meter. Pushed against the wall was a kitchen table with leaves that folded down when not in use, and four chairs.

The half-glazed kitchen door opened into the back garden, which resembled a ploughed field when we first moved in but was soon laid with paths and a shed for garden tools. Wire link fences divided the gardens and at the far end were well-established hedges and trees, belonging to the houses backing on to ours, the fronts of which faced the main village street.

Leading from the kitchen a door to the side of the larder opened into a lounge and dining room that spanned the width of the house from front to back with a window at each end. In the middle of the central wall was an unimaginative, dull, grey, tiled fireplace with a small grate, that burned coke to heat the back boiler and in turn the water. On the floor were hard, black, composition tiles, which were cold and constantly needed polishing. A door at the front end of the lounge opened into a square hall encompassing the front door with frosted glass panels, and the staircase leading to a large landing from which three bedrooms and a bathroom led off.

At last, we all had our own space. I had quite a large bedroom, which I was only too happy to keep clean and tidy. It also meant that for the first time I was able to keep my own personal toys and dolls in my room instead of altogether in the toy box. My brother was given the box room, which he never seemed to keep tidy, and my parents had the large bedroom that housed the airing cupboard. All the windows were large with tiled sills, the curtains coloured and patterned to suit our individual tastes (the first time we children had been allowed to choose anything of our own).

I don't remember ever being particularly happy there. Certainly my mother never really liked the place, even though it was supposed to be modern in comparison to the cottage, but she did her best to make it as nice and homely as possible.

The village school was a five-minute walk along the main street, an old mid-Victorian building with one large classroom and one small one. The headmaster and his wife were the two main teachers, assisted by a part-time teacher who helped with some of the recreational activities such as painting, dancing and games. The toilets were in an alley outside, adjacent to the cricket and recreational field and the village hall.

The hall, occasionally used by the school for games and country dancing, had a large dining room to the side, where, I remember, on one occasion I was forced to eat cabbage! Our food was served to us and we weren't allowed to leave any on our plates. The headmaster would supervise the lunches, pacing up and down between the rows of tables, hands clasped behind his back, beady eyes on everyone. If any food was left on a plate he would stand over the poor, frightened child until every morsel was eaten and the plate clean. Intimidation after the style of Oliver Twist! On the particular day in question, unaware that the cabbage was slimy and overcooked, I accepted it onto my plate but then found I was totally unable to swallow it. After standing over me for some time with a cane held behind his back, the headmaster suggested that the whole school would stay until I had finished my meal. I tried to force some cabbage down. Retching, and with my stomach heaving, I was eventually sick all over the dinner plate, much to his disgust. He never stood behind me again and I never, ever had school cabbage again.

I have mixed memories about the school. Some things, like the milk bottles lined up warming on the huge old iron radiators in the winter, the skipping games in the playground, the country dancing in the hall, and the outdoor art lessons at which I seemed to excel, are all good memories. Others, like coats hanging in the freezing cloakroom, often still soaking wet when it was time to go home, the freezing cold toilets and the school dinners, are certainly not happy ones!

I made lots of friends in the new village and one person who stood out as a real character was the village 'bobby'. He was friendly and respected by everyone, and all the children loved him, even though they knew that if they were up to any mischief he would not hesitate to give them a swift clip round the ear. It was amazing just how well behaved everyone was when he was walking around and, to get anywhere in a hurry, he had a police bicycle.

Once we'd moved house, my father didn't go poaching quite as often but he'd kept his coat and gun. Some local boys had a pet jackdaw and at some time or other they must have upset my father. I discovered he had a sadistic streak when, one day as the jackdaw was sitting on the roof, cawing and squawking, my father aimed his gun at it and fired. The bird fell to the ground. The boys were heartbroken on discovering their pet was dead and, although they had their suspicions as to the perpetrator, no one actually confronted my father and he never owned up to the crime. This incident raised suspicions in my mind about our pet rabbits, who would 'escape' from time to time, usually around new year when we would dine on rabbit stew.

My mother seemed to have less patience these days, often left alone while Father was away working whilst at the same time trying to run the home, look after us and keep up the cleaning jobs she'd taken on. If we were naughty or got into mischief, she would whip us round the legs or backside, using a cane that was conveniently kept beside the cooker. This was pretty frightening and not only did it sting but left weals on the skin. My brother and I soon learned that if we were quick enough we could get beyond the reach of the cane or the lashings if we got under the dining table.

It was then a waiting game to see who gave up first, or who could get out without her noticing, and escape to the bedroom and lock themselves in. We still got a caning, but it was delayed!

Not long after moving house, when I must have been about eight years old and my brother would have been five, I experienced the first Christmas that would be permanently etched into my memory.

It was a bright, sunny Christmas Day. The house was decorated with the traditional paper chains, hanging in loops from the central light to the edges of the room like bent spokes in a wheel. We had sat for hours making the coloured strips, and then glueing them daisy chain fashion. In the corners of the room groups of balloons swung from ties, a few of which had already begun leaking air and started to look soft. A decorated tree stood in the corner of the lounge, its pine needles soundlessly dropped and scattered on the floor beneath. The tree looked very pretty when its fairy lights were switched on.

There was no ceremony about the opening of Christmas presents in our house. They were placed in a pillowcase, which was then put at the bottom of our beds sometime during Christmas Eve, and we would just open them when we woke up. I had long ago given up on the idea that Father Christmas delivered presents to every child in every house, in every street, town, village and country throughout the world. It always amazed me that any child with an ounce of intelligence could still be naïve enough to not work out that it would take more than one night for Santa to deliver presents to even one town, let alone the whole world. Even so, we all pretended that Santa could perform this miracle, so as not to spoil it for my brother. My parents would usually open their presents whilst drinking an early morning cup of tea in bed.

Later on we played out with friends and some of the other children in the street who were trying out new bicycles and roller skates. Having fallen over several times whilst practising these new skills, we went back indoors to enjoy quieter, less painful activities.

Around midday my brother and I were playing with some of our new presents on the hearthrug in front of the fire. The fireplace was piled to one side with stacked logs and on the other side stood the rack with the fire irons. The fire was too small for the large room and, as we sat near it, parts of us got hot, and burned and scorched, while other parts were left to chill.

Smells wafted through the house from the kitchen as dinner cooked in the oven. My mother was having to use considerable skill this Christmas, as this was all fairly new to her. She was used to the primitive cooking facilities at the cottage and, though the modern gas cooker was especially wonderful, Christmas dinner for the four of us was still quite something. Up until now, Christmas had always been spent with my grandparents but Mother had looked forward to doing everything herself this year. This was to be the first Christmas the four of us would spend on our own.

Father was out visiting, taking small tokens of appreciation to his customers (people for whom he did small private decorating jobs to bring in extra income, which subsidised a rather poorly paid job he managed to get at the town hospital). A car drew up outside the house but we took no notice until there was a knock on the door. My brother and I dashed to the window and looked out to see who was there. Mother went to the front door, tea towel still in hand and, on hearing her exclamation of surprise, we dashed to the door to see who it was. My father's eldest brother and sister, and their respective spouses, had decided to come out of London, on a twenty-six mile drive, to show off their new car. Added to that was the excuse that they had come to see their little brother's new home.

They were all ushered into the sitting room and we were smothered with hugs and kisses before they eventually sat down. It was very unusual for any of the family to visit us. We were the ones to visit, taking a Green Line bus to visit family in East Ham in London's East End. These were great outings for us, dressing up, going into the nearby market town to catch the bus, a single-decker express to Walthamstow. Once there, we would catch a connection to Forest Gate for the last stage of the journey, which, if we were really lucky, would mean a ride on a trolley bus.

We could tell from the look on Mother's face and by her actions that not only was she surprised but also none too pleased at this sudden intrusion by in-laws without invitation or warning. She appeared to be flustered and unsure how to entertain them in Father's absence. She explained that he was out and was expected back soon, so she offered them a drink. Expecting to make tea or coffee, she was a bit taken aback by the request for whisky, gin and sherry, and, knowing the family to be heavy drinkers, she kept the measures small.

A look of relief came over her as, luckily, Father arrived back from his visits before too long and was greeted with big hugs, pats on the back and handshakes from the relatives, and a glare from my mother. He was delighted to see them all and this gave Mother the opportunity to escape to the kitchen to check on the food and top up the steamer under the Christmas pudding.

Father never needed any encouragement to drink and without hesitation promptly poured one for himself and refilled the guests' glasses far more generously than Mother had done. From the smell of him when he came in it was obvious he'd already had several 'last ones for the road' during his visits. In his family's company the conversation was difficult to understand and follow, and even my mother, who had picked up quite a lot along the way, didn't understand the broad Cockney language. The men, in particular, spoke in Cockney rhyming slang. The chatter got noisy and party-like and, although the indication had been that they would not be stopping long, they continued to drink and chat and joke. I could see Mother getting more and more exasperated, pacing backwards and forwards to the kitchen. It was nearly time to serve the dinner and the visitors showed no sign of leaving. On the contrary, they looked settled for the day.

I don't know whether Mother managed to signal to Father or if he went to the kitchen of his own accord, but when he did leave the party and they were both away from the guests, we could hear angry whispers and heated exchanges taking place. My brother and I were getting hungry and the smells wafting in from the kitchen were really making my tummy rumble. We could hear pots and pans being banged around and the kitchen door had been slammed shut. Voices were being raised, and still the visitors stayed.

Father returned to the sitting room and one of the aunts asked if she could use the bathroom. This gave my father the opportunity to show the family over the rest of the house and garden. When they had left the room by the far door into the hall, Mother came in from the kitchen and asked me to help lay up the table. She was looking more flustered and I could see she was getting into a state. With a look of pure fury, she threw the tablecloth over the dining table. I remember it was a particularly beautiful Christmas cloth of white linen, that Mother had embroidered with holly and mistletoe. She had sat for hours working on it, and was so proud when it was finished.

We could hear the laughing and joking going on upstairs and the noise of heavy feet as they moved from room to room. Either I didn't hear what I was told or I misunderstood, but after getting out cutlery for four, Mother said I needed to lay the table for eight. I was about to question this but after one look at her face the question died on my lips. We didn't have eight dining chairs so the kitchen chairs would have to be brought in. Did we have enough plates and cutlery? I wondered. Even at the tender age of eight, I knew something was dreadfully wrong and, although Mother was fuming, she seemed resigned to the fact that we had unexpected, uninvited quests, who would be stretching her resources to the limit.

The table was laid with extra placemats and glasses, the candles and centrepiece put in place, and crackers laid at each setting, together with a paper napkin at the side. Even though it was cramped, it looked pretty.

The lengthy guided tour around upstairs was completed with a great deal of jollity, and Mother announced that the turkey was ready to be carved. It was traditional for the man to carve any large joint at Sunday lunch or on special occasions, so Father always did the carving.

I feel sure my mother expected the family to excuse themselves at this stage, protesting that they had not come expecting to be fed. Instead, it seemed that with the table ready laid and waiting for a meal to be served, they all took this as an open invitation to take a seat and tuck in. One aunt was looking slightly uncomfortable and seemed about to make a comment but a prod and a harsh look from my uncle kept her quiet.

Somehow, with a great deal of embarrassment and certainly no apologies, Mother served up eight meals from a small turkey and vegetables prepared for four people. The men were given bottles of beer to go with the meal, the women preferred shandy, and my brother and I had lemonade. Whether or not the dinners were considered to be on the small side, we never knew, but every plate was cleared. During the meal, the tension between my parents was sizzling, but Father and his family carried on the banter almost mockingly. However, no one raised a single comment about the gate-crashing of our Christmas Day. My brother and I contributed little to the conversation since we were expected to 'only speak when spoken to' when in company, and we knew it. A strict disciplinarian, Father believed that children were meant to be 'seen and not heard' so at the dining table we would sit in silence—no conversation, just the sound of cutlery hitting the crockery and the chewing and chopping of food. We were also taught never to interrupt and to respect our elders.

When the plates had been cleared, the Christmas pudding, which had been steaming all morning, was turned out onto a large dish, set on fire in the middle of the table with ceremonial brandy flame, and served with custard. We were warned to watch out for the lucky threepenny bits that had been stirred into the mixture before cooking. (I assume they were found by the visitors, since they were the only lucky ones that day!) Finally, tea was served to wash it all down.

Whilst the three women helped in the kitchen with the washing up, the men sat on the settee and went to sleep. My brother and I played on the floor and tried to keep quiet so as not to disturb their noisy snores or attract attention. The afternoon wore on. More drinks were poured, the fire made up and, as the light faded, curtains were drawn, lights turned on and the Christmas tree lit up in all its splendour. And still they stayed.

My poor mother. I couldn't believe how tired and harassed she looked. She was not enjoying this Christmas Day one little bit. It was obvious to me that this was far from the original plan, playing the unwilling hostess to unexpected relatives who didn't even have the decency to make a contribution to the day, having brought nothing with them.

It was some time before anyone realised that Mother had been gone for a while. Retreating to the kitchen, she was preparing a suppertime snack since it was now early evening and there was still no sign of the visitors preparing to leave. She had probably decided she would just have to continue to make the best of it.

The dining table was laid with sandwiches, pickles, mince pies, sausage rolls and, in the centre on a raised pedestal glass dish, Mother's homemade Christmas cake. More drinks were poured and everyone tucked into the buffet, with my brother and I being made to sit at the table as we weren't trusted not to make a mess on the floor!

The food quickly disappeared, the cake was cut, and what appeared to be jollity and laughter continued well into the evening. Before it got too late, my father said, 'Right kids, time to get ready for shuteye. Time to say goodnight to everyone and take a ball up the apples.' (Ball of chalk, walk; apples and pears, stairs.) We were well aware of this Cockney expression and prepared for the fuss of saying goodbye—kisses all round, pats on heads, exchanges of 'see you again soon' and 'lovely to see you'. The uncles turned out their pockets, and small change and a shiny half-crown was given to each of us.

By the time the family left we were asleep and unaware of their departure. Next morning we listened to the raised voices, angry exchanges and the front door slamming when my father left the house. My brother and I washed and dressed, cleaned our teeth and made our beds, but stayed upstairs, afraid to go down, as we often were when our parents were arguing. Eventually, Mother called for us to get up or go without breakfast.

Mother had obviously been up and about for quite a while. The grate had been cleared, the fire rekindled and lit, the sitting room had been tidied and dusted, borrowed furniture returned to the kitchen which itself had been restored to its normal neatness with everything in place. She looked puffy-eyed and pale, as if she had been crying.

After a breakfast of porridge and warm milk, my brother and I went out to play. We were instructed not to go far and to be back in time for lunch. We played with friends and children who were visiting relatives and staying over the Christmas holidays. We shared all the delights of new toys and chatted about Christmas, parties, visitors and any funny things that had taken place over the holiday.

Around midday, we made our way home and cleaned up for lunch. Mother was strangely quiet (my father didn't appear to have returned), and she was laying the table. Lunch consisted of slices of boiled ham, mashed potatoes and parsnips, with Mother muttering that there were no leftovers from Christmas Day due to unexpected visitors. She herself didn't eat much, she just picked at her meal, and when we had eaten she cleared away, washed up and went upstairs to lie down.

I don't remember much about the rest of the day, but I do remember going to bed and then being woken up when my father arrived home late and drunk, falling over things trying to find his way into the house. No one knew where he had been all day, and so a new argument erupted. Father was unable to make it up the stairs so he stayed where he was and woke up on the hearth mat in front of a cold and burnt-out grate.

For days after, and into the new year, the atmosphere was dreadful. Mother snapped at us. Father came in late every evening to warmed-up food, very little of which he ate. My brother and I just kept out of the way. Our parents didn't utter a word to each other for days, other than to throw insults, refresh old arguments or to hold slanging matches. We were glad to be returning to school, back into a more normal existence.

Things at home managed to drift slowly back to 'normal' by about March (my birthday month) and months later, whilst at the hairdressers with my mother and brother, I learned in more detail what had taken place during that dreadful Christmas period.

The hairdresser, a lovely lady who used the back room of her bungalow for her work, was saying to my mother, 'Goodness, I can't believe that it will soon be Christmas again. It only seems like yesterday that we were celebrating the last one. What are you doing this year, or haven't you thought about it yet?'

My mother replied, 'After last Christmas, I haven't given it a thought, I'm dreading it, but I do know that I won't be put on and caught out like that again.'

'Why, what happened?' asked the hairdresser.

'My husband's thoughtless family had the nerve to turn up uninvited, without a thought for whether we had enough food, and stayed well into the night. We had no turkey left for Boxing Day, they drank all the booze, and they didn't bring anything with them by way of contribution.'

'Oh dear,' said the hairdresser, 'did you have no idea at all?'

'None,' said my mother, 'and to make matters worse, I was accused of not making his family welcome. It was as if, somehow, I could spirit food out of mid-air and should have welcomed them with open arms.' She went on, 'They had drunk so much by the time they left that none of them could walk straight, but they all got into the new car, which was their excuse to call in the first place, and managed to get back to London in one piece. How, I will never know. It was the new car that they really wanted to show off, that was the reason for the ride out.'

The hairdresser agreed, 'It was a bit of a cheek. You would have expected them to at least let you know. Some people are so thoughtless. You wouldn't have the nerve, would you?'

Mother continued, 'My husband and I had a terrible row. He went to visit friends on Boxing Day and arrived home rolling drunk. I was made to feel that it was all my fault.'

'Typical man,' said the hairdresser, 'he wouldn't have the foggiest idea about making food go round and preparing in advance.'

'What would you have done under the circumstances?' my mother asked, and, without waiting for a reply, continued, 'I couldn't leave the dinner to ruin. I didn't have time to prepare any more, and I didn't have enough really, so I shared it out as best I could which left us with very little for the next day.'

The hairdresser, who was a friend of both my parents, said,

'What will you do to prevent it happening again?'

'I don't think my husband will let it happen again but, if it did, I will be more prepared. I will just turn off the cooker and tell them the dinner is in the oven. Me and the kids will go to my mum's,' said Mother resolutely.

# CHAPTER 6
## Drunken Christmas

Things moved on. My father started up in business on his own and we moved again, this time to a small market town and a house which Father had been to see briefly, then purchased at auction with money borrowed from my grandfather.

The house was in need of repair and modernisation, but it was in a nice area on a main road, with its own front gate, front door, path to the back garden and an entrance to the rear of the garden through a small cul-de-sac. Although impressive-looking from the outside it had no bathroom, no heating and no hot water, and so it seemed as though we were moving back in time rather than forwards. It had potential, although you needed a lot of imagination and enthusiasm to see it. It was just ten minutes' walk from the town centre, set on a bus route, and fifteen minutes walk from the railway station, with trains directly to London and Cambridge.

Mother had not seen the house, she was only taken to view it after the purchase had taken place. We went to clear the place out about a week before moving in. My first impression was how dark and dowdy it was, with a musty smell, high ceilings and dark wallpaper and paintwork. The kitchen had no fittings, just an old butler sink standing on blocks and a cold water tap. The toilet was in a lean-to shed outside at the end of the kitchen, with a high, rusting water tank and a wooden handle on a long chain to pull for flushing. We were back in time and motion, to chamber pots and cold outings to the toilet.

The cupboard in the kitchen was full of jars of mouldy jam, pickles, sauces, home-made preserves of fruit and vegetables, all of which were quickly thrown away. The rooms were full of cobwebs and, in places, the dull and discoloured wallpaper was coming away from the walls. The bedrooms contained old clothes, tea chests and cardboard boxes full of junk, the linoleum-covered floors scraped and torn. The threadbare stair carpet was so dangerous it needed removing. At the end of the day we were filthy, dirty and exhausted.

After moving in my parents found it difficult to adjust to the new, and very different, environment. Initially moving from a very quiet village to a housing estate well away from the high street, we were now living on a main road with heavy traffic night and day, making it very difficult to sleep. During the harvest season and from October to December, heavy lorries thundered along the road at all times, transporting grain to the mills and sugar beet to the refinery factory a few miles away. At that time this was the main route from the East End of London to Cambridge, and therefore very busy.

Modernisation of the house took more than seven years (my mother never expected to live long enough to see it completed!). Initially, and working at quite a pace, the most important jobs were tackled. The outside toilet was demolished and an extension built at the end of the kitchen to serve as a bathroom. The kitchen itself was gutted and refitted. Electrical rewiring was carried out and a solid fuel, coke-burning boiler installed to heat water and radiators. Lack of time and money meant that the lounge and bedrooms waited quite a while before being modernised. Father did most of the building work himself and only used professionals for electrical and plumbing work.

I was about ten when we moved to this house. I attended an elite, posh church school but, as I was only going to be there for two terms, I was excused from having to wear the required uniform. The move also meant that we were now within walking distance of large shops and department stores, and on market day the town was extremely busy. The bustling streets and market traders caused hold-ups and traffic jams, which I found all very thrilling. More importantly, once we'd moved to the town, I then had access to double-decker buses.

The previous spring my grandparents had moved to my great-grandmother's house, in order to help care for her in her own home. I'm sure they agonised and soul-searched a great deal over this decision but, once made, they moved, lock, stock and barrel, to a town that, although only ten miles away, seemed like another world in those days when little or no transport was available. To me, they might just as well have been a hundred miles away. But, in moving, we now lived on a main road where there was a bus stop fifty yards along the way for trips into town. Opposite this was the bus stop to the neighbouring town, and to my grandparents!

There was, however, one bonus from their moving. There was no room for their piano at Great-Grandmother's house, so it was left at ours. I gazed in awe at the shining, walnut body and tinkered with its ivory keys. It was decided that I could start piano lessons, to which I looked forward with both trepidation and excitement.

Now that we lived in a town, we began to move into a more sophisticated and upmarket way of life. Poaching and hunting out of necessity were things of the past (the gun had long gone) and pheasants, hares and rabbits now arrived as gifts. As well as being self-employed, my father had also become well known in the circles of small businessmen and joined the local British Legion Club. To become a member you needed an introduction by an existing member, and this came about after he joined a team of builders and decorators carrying out a large maintenance contract on a big local hotel.

The Club was held in a large Victorian building with a large bar area, a large games room and a big family room. It always struck me as being a dark, sleazy place, smelling of stale tobacco and usually filled with a smoky haze. Wives and girlfriends were not generally allowed on the premises. Occasionally, family events were held to which wives, girlfriends and children were invited and which, for the most part, were great fun.

Throughout the year there were prize-giving parties at which trophies were handed out to the winners of pool, snooker and darts competitions.

There was an annual seaside outing that usually required the use of three or four coaches, on which were loaded crates of drink, mothers with picnic baskets packed full of goodies, and children carrying buckets and spades, and who would return laden with the usual traditional extras such as balloons, goggles and kiss-me-quick hats.

One event, which was particularly great fun, was the special bonfire night party and firework display. Bar-b-qued steaks, sausages and chops, hot oven-cooked potatoes—all served in the grounds with drinks all round. On this occasion the children ran riot in the games room and around the bar once the fireworks were over. When the adults had put up with enough of the noise, the fighting, running around, smacks, tears, and frayed tempers, the proprietor would bang the gong and suggest that 'the party is over' and call 'time'.

Another party evening would be held on the night of the local pantomime, and Club members would make a block booking at the local theatre and then meet up at the club afterwards.

However, special events and occasions aside, the company and some of the goings-on at this club were a bit smutty, to say the least. It didn't take my father long to fall in with some of the bad elements of the clan, getting involved in regular drinking binges and usually coming home very late for meals, often the worse for drink.

Not long after becoming a member a really awful row broke out between my parents, after my mother had found some photographs in one of Father's jacket pockets. At first he denied they were his, insisting that he was looking after them for a mate. Eventually, it came to light that the photos had been hidden away in his old army bag, and he had been showing them to colleagues at the British Legion Club.

The photos, pornographic pictures in the worst possible taste, were taken in Italy while my father had been posted there with the army. My mother was horrified and couldn't believe what she was seeing. They pictured women in compromising positions with animals and were particularly disgusting. It made my father very popular with the men at the club but it made my mother wonder what went on while he was in Italy and she was at home, pregnant with me. My mother had heard stories of people's sexual antics with animals on farms, but she had never come across bestiality and was sickened by it. She threatened to burn the pictures but my father turned on her and told her he would sell them if it would make her happy. She told him she didn't care what happened to them as long as they were not in the house. I think this whole incident played on my mother's mind for a long time.

Christmas finally arrived after weeks of preparation. Three or four days before Christmas, Father would go to the Christmas auction held in the corn exchange building, where large joints of meat, game and poultry were sold, and where he would purchase the best bargains for the Christmas table. He also purchased considerable amounts of beer and alcohol through the British Legion Club at a good discount. Several of his customers would bestow boxes of wines and spirits on him. The remainder of the shopping, including the presents (as well as her own from my father) was bought by Mother.

I'd helped Mother to do the shopping and make the mincemeat,

Christmas puddings and Christmas cake. We made our own decorations and streamers, and wrapped presents to put under the tree.

On Christmas morning, instead of the usual pile of presents in the bedroom, all the presents were under the tree and we were allowed to open one present each with breakfast. My parents had decided that the rest would be kept until after the Christmas dinner and the Queen's speech, so that it could be a leisurely affair with all the family together.

The turkey had been put in the oven very early that morning, before my brother and I were awake, and we later helped to prepare the vegetables and get things ready for the meal. The pudding was put on to steam for the required six hours, and my mother had a timetable to work through so that it could all go like clockwork and everything would be ready on time.

My father had diaries ready to distribute to his customers and he was preparing to go out on his rounds. He also took out unpaid invoices as he thought it may have more impact on Christmas morning and make the defaulters pay up. My mother had insisted that he should be home by two o'clock or the dinner would be ruined. When he left they were both in a lovey-dovey mood and everything seemed fine.

Throughout the morning I helped to make the table look special and made special napkin rings, crackers and a table decoration. There was mistletoe hanging in the doorway, and the sideboard was dressed with a special runner on which lay a tray with glasses and bowls filled with nuts and fruit, the likes of which we didn't normally see. There were also boxes of chocolates, liqueurs and crystallised fruits, some of which were presents to my mother from her employers and regular hotel guests (she had found work as a chambermaid at the hotel my father had been working on when they had advertised for staff).

As the morning passed we basted the turkey, put potatoes and parsnips in to roast and prepared the giblets for the gravy. My mother had a brief visit from a neighbour and they had a glass of sherry each for the seasonal exchange of good cheer. When the neighbour left, the final preparations for the meal were made and the vegetables put on ready to cook. The dinner was almost ready for serving and, with no sign of my father arriving, the atmosphere began to get tense. Two o'clock came and went. Still my father hadn't arrived and things were getting fraught. Mother was getting annoyed, pacing the room and checking the oven. Everything was put on as low a heat as possible to delay any chance of burning. Finally, my mother lost her temper. My brother discreetly disappeared up to his bedroom. We were all hungry and the smell of the cooking was just making things worse. My mother removed the turkey from the oven and did something that was just not allowed in our family—she carved the turkey. This had always been Father's job as head of the household, but now Mother attacked the roasted bird with the carving knife and fork, as if she was slicing meat off my father. Venting her anger on this large, succulent, stuffed bird with relish, she laid the meat on a large heated plate. I was the only one in the firing line so she took her frustration out on me. Suddenly, she burst out, 'I'll swing for your father. He just can't be trusted. Once he gets out with his friends he forgets there is a family waiting at home.'

I just kept quiet. What could I say in response? She carried on, 'He's so selfish, he never considers anyone but himself. It's alright for him, gallivanting and living a life of Riley, while I'm stuck here, slaving away in the kitchen all morning. He'll probably walk through the door, all sweetness and light, and wonder what the fuss is all about.'

I was looking out of the window, to the end of the garden. Skeletal shadows fell across the barren earth where the vegetables had once been, cast by the sun shining through the bare tree branches. Mother was busy doing un-Christmas things, like little odd jobs, to try and keep from getting more upset over another awkward situation.

How well she knew my father. It was four o'clock in the afternoon and getting dusk. I saw the van draw up at the bottom of the garden. I watched as its door was opened and he almost fell out onto the path. I was beginning to feel afraid. We never knew what to expect when he arrived home in that state. The amazing thing was that he managed to drive home at all. How did he do it? He eventually staggered round to the rear doors of the van and tried to remove a box. He made several attempts, nearly dropped it, appeared to reconsider the manoeuvre, pushed it back inside the van and locked the doors.

If the situation had not been so serious, it would have been funny. He staggered down the steps, twice going back onto the foot which was on the higher step, before eventually finding the ground level of the garden path, grabbing hold of the washing line post to steady himself. It was like watching a circus clown fool around in the ring for the children's delight, the sad part being that, unless the neighbours were covertly peeping through their curtains, I was the only one observing this performance. He staggered from left to right, missed his step, slipped onto the garden, regained control and tried to walk a straight line to the back door. He did quite well until the dustbin got in his way and, with a loud clatter amid a few choice expletives, he pulled himself up to his full height and stood on the doorstep for a while to prepare himself for his entrance.

Mother had witnessed part of this fiasco and, fuming, sat herself on a chair, her face red with anger. I sat down and awaited the onslaught, my heart thumping in my chest so loudly I thought everyone could hear it. The door opened slightly, then closed again while Father, swaying from side to side, tried to regain his balance. The door opened slightly again but this time Mother was on her feet and, like a shot, grabbed the door handle and pulled it back so hard that my father seemed to be catapulted into the room, still hanging onto the door handle on the other side. Even in his drunken stupor, the look of surprise and amazement was clear to see, as he fell first onto my mother and then against the wall. He then attempted to throw his arms around Mother's neck but she pushed him away and, with hands on hips, she could contain herself no longer.

'How dare you? What time do you call this? You have a funny idea of two o'clock,' she exploded.

'Oh, c'mon, luv, itsh Chrishmash. Give ush a kish,' my father replied, as he staggered against the wall.

'I'll give you "it's Christmas". The dinner, our CHRISTMAS DINNER, is ruined thanks to you,' Mother burst out.

My father began to approach her and, as he did so, she picked up the carving knife, pointed it towards him, and said, 'Don't you dare come near me in that drunken state. You are a disgrace.'

From where I sat, this pantomime was hilarious, but I wasn't laughing, I was terrified. I had seen things like this before, and I was wishing I had made my escape upstairs earlier. Too late now, so I just had to sit tight and see it through.

Father laughed at my mother. He staggered around trying to get his coat off, one arm in and one arm out, he bounced around between the door and the wall. Although he had some compre-hension of what was happening, he was too drunk to absorb what Mother was saying or to realise just how angry she was.

The drama continued for a while, with my mother throwing insults and Father behaving like the drunken idiot he was, until he staggered back, lost his footing and fell over the arm of, and into, a chair. Raising his head, he looked at me with glazed eyes and a stupid smile on his face. He looked like the village idiot. He just slumped where he was and fell asleep. I felt real hate for my father whenever he was in this condition, and the awful stench of stale whisky and dirty ashtrays is something I detest to this day.

My mother was furious. She yelled up the stairs for my brother to come down if he wanted anything to eat and he quickly appeared from the top of the stairs, where he had been cowering and listening for some time. He looked cold and frightened. It's funny how hunger seems to ease when fright takes over and, although we had not eaten since breakfast, we could have easily managed without food for quite a bit longer. However, Mother decided we had waited long enough and dished up four dinners, setting three over steamers to be reheated and leaving the fourth on the side.

The spirit of Christmas was now somewhat lacking. Father continued to sit slumped in the chair with a silly grin fixed on his face. The food looked appetising and smelled delicious. My brother and I tucked in but Mother, after all the effort that had gone into preparing this one big meal of the year, could only pick at her meal. Though obviously still very angry, she appeared to be deep in thought. Eventually she pushed her plate away and burst out crying. Through the tears and the sniffles she let loose a tirade towards my father:

'You bastard! You drunken slob! This is the second Christmas over the last few years that you've ruined. You treat me no better than a servant. I refuse to be treated like this by you. You are never going to do this to me again, I'll see to that.' Little did she know.

Father was now snoring loudly, having adjusted his position in the chair, with the silly grin still set on his face and oblivious to all around him. The crackers remained un-pulled on the table, the candles unlit, the presents still wrapped beneath the tree. My father slept through, unaware of the hurt, upset, torment and humiliation his family suffered as a result of his thoughtless selfishness. Mother pulled herself together, my brother and I rallied and cleared the table. The washing up was done and the three of us went to bed.

As Boxing Day dawned all was quiet in the house. I listened in trepidation for the slightest sound. As I sat in bed with my dressing gown around my shoulders and reading a book, I looked out at the weather, wondering what this day would hold for us all.

Mother was the first to get up and I heard her go downstairs and begin to get breakfast ready. I then got up, so did my brother, and we got on with the usual chores. Very little was said at breakfast, and of Father there was no sign. Once breakfast was over and cleared away, we were told we could open the presents that remained under the tree. We could hear Father moving around upstairs and when he finally appeared in the dining room, he behaved as if nothing was any different to usual, although he still looked hung over. He didn't eat any breakfast, just took a cup of tea, and the deathly silence he faced in the kitchen was to continue for another few days, creating yet again a dreadful atmosphere that no child should have to live in. Not for the first time, my brother and I were glad to get back to school after the holiday, and listen to stories of how other children spent their Christmas.

# CHAPTER 7
## Mai Ling

By the time I was fourteen, Father had become a well-established and sought-after joiner and decorator, not just in the town but in some of the larger houses and establishments further afield. On more than one occasion, he travelled as far away as Scotland and Cornwall with two or three workmates, to carry out large and extensive contracts obtained on the recommendations of local clients. Some of his more wealthy clients offered perks, such as their holiday homes for us to take our holidays.

Imagining himself to be of great importance, Father tried to become a member of the Freemasons. He had lots of drinking pals and friends who either belonged to the police force or who were magistrates or businessmen, and he considered himself to be moving in the right circles. He believed he was well liked and accepted by these people, but someone obviously didn't like him. I remember him coming home one evening very drunk, announcing that he had been 'blackballed'. At that time I wasn't aware of the importance of this announcement, but it was a clear sign that somebody in his band of 'friends' did not approve of him, so much so that he was not allowed to become a member of the secret society. He was utterly dismayed at being excluded from the Freemasons. It was a real jolt to his enormous ego, which took him a long time to come to terms with. My mother was not only relieved but secretly delighted to think that someone had got the better of my father and, for once, he hadn't been able to make an impact, or a good one at least, and get his own way.

Father's character led him to become known as a loveable rogue. People, particularly women, would say he could charm the birds off the trees, and it was true—he could. He also had the knack of making money out of anything that crossed his path. He could always 'get things' for people at knockdown prices, and always knew where to get rid of anything that 'fell off the back of a lorry'. As a black market trader, forever doing deals involving booze, paint, tools, and a variety of other items, he was always in demand. Father was also the life and soul of any party, knowing how to drink with the best of them, sing (he had a very good voice), and always able to tell a good joke!

However, the older I got, the more I came to know the other side of the man, and the heartache and pain he had caused my mother since they first married. Even at school I'd heard rumours about my father from girls who'd had boyfriends working with him, but I either dismissed or ignored them, perhaps wishing they weren't true, but realising deep down that they probably were. The Christmas of that year, one of those that haunts me most, was to prove them all true.

On Christmas Eve my brother and I were helping with the last minute preparations. Most of the presents were wrapped, the final trimmings had been put on the Christmas tree, and it was getting quite late. This was the only evening of the whole year that I could stay up late, with no worries about oversleeping in the morning or being late for the paper round. So, I made the most of it. We had an extra-large turkey this year so Mother was going to cook it very slowly on a low heat throughout the night. She had just covered it with foil and put it in the oven when we heard footsteps coming down the path and then voices outside the back door.

The door was opened by my father, who then stood to one side to allow a tall, slim, smiling beauty to step inside. My mother froze on the spot. She glared at the young woman, an oriental with jet black hair and very dark eyes. Beautifully made up and her clothes fitting like a skin, she carried a holdall with both hands in front of her and a shoulder bag swayed by her side. She wore a dark cape, which hung loosely around her shoulders. The embroidery on her blouse sparkled every bit as much as her jewellery and hair clip. With her hand outstretched as she approached my mother to greet her, my father announced, 'This is Mai Ling.' I watched the colour drain from my mother's face as she stood there, paralysed with shock, stunned into silence. Quickly pulling herself together, and without offering her hand in return, Mother glared at my father and asked, 'And just who is Mai Ling?'

Although he rarely worked at the local hospital now, Father still kept in contact with many of the people he'd met whilst working there. Work carried out at the hospital often meant long hours, i.e. late nights or all night, and weekend working, so that wards and operating theatres requiring work to be done were closed for the shortest possible time. These times were ideal opportunities for Father to engage in one of his favourite pastimes. Father had been drinking and in his usual, familiar, jovial drunken way, casually replied, 'She's a friend of mine, a nurse at the hospital.'

I looked first at the woman, and then at my father, with mounting horror. The shock was compounded more by the fact that Father was an out-and-out racist—not just anti-black, coloured, Indian, African or any other race, but he even disliked the Scots, Welsh and Irish people. He was a hypocrite. He could mix easily with Scots and Italians when it meant work, money and sex. And now, here in our own home, a Chinese beauty! As I continued to stare at her, I thought she was both beautiful and elegant but, at the same time, I hated her. How dare she?

My brother and I looked at each other, neither of us knowing how to react or what to say.

As she moved into the room, Mai Ling looked around and took everything in before turning to us both and, in broken English, said, 'Are you all ready for Christmas? The tree is very pretty. Your father has told me all about you.'

I looked at her and thought, I bet he has, and I bet that's not all he's told you either. I looked at my brother again, he looked at me, and we both looked at our parents. To prevent us from responding Mother promptly said it was getting late and that my brother should get to bed. He couldn't get out of the room quick enough and, with a collective goodnight, shot off up the stairs.

Father took Mai Ling's cape and offered her a seat. She gracefully moved to sit on a straight-backed chair and then crossed her legs. Father went to the sideboard and began pouring drinks. My mother had gone to the far side of the room to sit in an easy chair so that she could look directly at the visitor. I saw her eyes narrow, and felt the hate emanating from her towards this stranger and my father. Butterflies in my stomach accompanied the anticipation of yet another distasteful performance about to take place.

Without asking her preference, Father gave Mai Ling a drink, handed one to my mother and gave me a sherry (which I was only allowed if well diluted with lemonade). Having poured himself a large neat whisky, he raised his glass and proposed a toast.

'Here's wishing us all a happy Christmas,' he said.

Father tipped his drink back in one go, Mother took a mouthful of hers and Mai Ling raised her glass and sipped. I just sipped mine, feeling very ill at ease, as though waiting for a bomb to drop. The room seemed airless and I began to wish that I too had been allowed to escape to my bed.

Mother said, 'Right, well, if you'll excuse me, I have work to do and I need to be up early in the morning so I must get on.'

With that, she left the room and headed for the kitchen. Mai Ling pulled her bag towards her across the floor, took out several items wrapped in Christmas paper and put them on the table. She looked up uncertainly at my father, as if she didn't know what to say.

Standing behind her, he put his hands on her shoulders as if to steady himself and said to Mother's retreating figure, 'Mai Ling has brought some presents for everyone.'

Mother turned, and headed back into the living room. 'Really,' she said. 'Well, I'm afraid we weren't expecting you so we have no presents in return.'

Although this all sounded very civilised, the sarcasm in Mother's response was unmistakable.

Mai Ling replied, 'That's alright. It was a spur of the moment thing when I knew I was coming to see you.'

Mother looked at her questioningly and said, 'Oh, and when was that then?'

Father looked quite uncomfortable and, forestalling Mai Ling's reply, quickly interjected, 'I thought we could ask Mai Ling to join us for Christmas dinner. She is on call over Christmas, miles away from her family, and she will be on her own.'

I waited with bated breath for Mother's reply and when she did answer, it was clear she was not going to take this lying down. She braced herself, visibly stiffening and clenching her fists. Moving towards my father, her eyes were bulging and her face red with fury, but as controlled and calmly as possible she said, 'You thought what? You must think I'm stupid. I recognise the perfume—you've been wearing it all week! And now, you not only expect me to put up with your running around with all your fancy women behind my back, but you want me to entertain them as well.'

Father started to interrupt. 'Oh, come on, love, don't be like that. Where's your Christmas spirit? We can't—'

Mother flew at him before he could finish. 'Don't you "come on, love" me. You'll be offering her my bed next. Get her out of here before I do something I might regret.'

Mai Ling appeared to ignore what had been said and, picking up the largest of parcels from the table, thrust the packet towards my mother, saying, 'I have bought this for you. Please have it.'

Mother was just flabbergasted and promptly pushed the packet back to the other side of the table. 'If you think buying me presents makes everything ok you are very much mistaken,' she retorted.

Father stepped forward, took the packet and ripped the paper off to reveal a ghastly, tasteless, deep red shallow dish decorated with black and gold Chinese patterns (similar to those seen in Chinese restaurants!). Father obviously liked the dish and, after placing it on the sideboard, began transferring fruit from another bowl into it, while Mother looked on. 'Thank you, Mai Ling. It's lovely,' he said.

I wondered how long it would be before Mother either threw something across the room or burst into tears. I didn't know what to do or say, and felt extremely uncomfortable. Here, one of the rumours I'd heard was coming to life in our living room. A rumour no longer, the truth was displayed before my very eyes. Unable to help my mother, I felt utterly useless. She was being made to look like a dummy by this completely outrageous situation. Father wouldn't be able to deny this at all. He appeared to have no idea whatsoever of how my mother must have been feeling, or of what he was doing to his family. He looked smug. Mai Ling looked uncomfortable and said, 'Perhaps we should go.'

Mother replied, 'Yes, what a good idea, why don't you?' and with that, turned and practically ran to the bathroom, went in and locked the door.

Mai Ling got up from her chair, looked at me and smiling sweetly said, 'Nice to meet you. Have a nice Christmas.'

My father was about to say something but she laid her hand on his arm and shook her head. She picked up her cape from the back of the chair and they both turned and prepared to leave, the presents still sitting on the table. Father put Mai Ling's cape round her shoulders for her and opened the back door.

With a backward glance at me, Father said, 'I'll talk to you later.'

I could hear the clip-clop of high heels on the path, and then they were gone. I hurried to the bathroom. I could hear Mother sobbing inside and called to her through the door. 'Mum, is there anything I can do?' I knocked on the door. 'You can come out now, they've gone.'

After a while, the sobs died down, the door opened and she came out looking broken and forlorn.

'How could he?' she said. 'I can't believe this. How can your father treat us like this?'

I tried to comfort her but she pushed me away. She always did her crying in private. Wiping her eyes and face, she blew her nose and told me to get ready for bed.

Her parting shot was, 'We'll see what tomorrow brings. Prepare yourself for anything.'

I kissed her goodnight on the cheek and climbed the stairs. 'What does she mean?' I thought. I felt empty and sad. My heart ached with the fear of what might be to come. I cried myself to sleep.

I grew up that night. I saw my father for what he really was. I couldn't believe that he would have the nerve to do this to his family, particularly as I knew this must have been planned. He and Mai Ling must have discussed this visit and at some point made a plan of action, dependent upon the family's response.

She couldn't have just produced presents out of the blue. Perhaps she thought we knew about her coming. Whatever, we never saw her again, but for weeks after Christmas Father would come home and taunt my mother by singing 'Please Release Me', a song about someone asking to be released from a dead, loveless marriage, so that they can be free to love someone else. It almost drove my mother insane!

# CHAPTER 8
## Another Heartbreaking Christmas

It was very early when I awoke. I had obviously had a very disturbed night's sleep as the bed was really rumpled. Normally I could get up and it wouldn't even look slept in. I smelt the turkey as it cooked, and heard movement in the kitchen so I knew Mother was already up and about. Unlikely to get any more rest now, I decided to get up, and made my way downstairs. Mother looked as if she hadn't slept at all, but was dressed and busy getting things ready. The vegetables, sausages and bacon rolls were laid out on the work surface ready to be prepared. With no real greeting between us, I just pecked her on the cheek with a 'Good morning, Mum. Merry Christmas.' I didn't really expect any response and got on with laying the table for breakfast. I asked if she would like some tea, and proceeded to fill the kettle and put the cups on the tray.

Mother continued busying herself, humming as she did so, nothing tuneful, just a nervous habit. Removing the turkey from the oven, she basted it, drained off some of the juices, turned the tray round and returned it to the oven. We sat together for our breakfast of tea and toast, making small talk, neither of us mentioning the events of the previous night.

After a while I left the table, cleared away and rinsed the dishes, and went into the living room to put a selection of fruit and nuts in bowls. Mother carried on, preparing the vegetables for dinner, and as I could hear no movement upstairs I suggested it was time to wake my brother.

As I climbed the stairs I wondered whether Father had got up really early and gone out, or if he was sleeping off a hangover. I stood outside my parents' bedroom and listened. No sounds of snoring or breathing were audible so I pushed opened the door just enough to be able to poke my head through. I was shocked to see the bed was already made and there was no evidence that Father had been in the room at all.

I went along to my brother's room and found him up and dressed, sitting on his bed making a Meccano model. I asked him to come downstairs to have his breakfast and then open some presents. He asked me if Dad was down there.

'No,' I replied. 'Did you hear him go out this morning?'

He shrugged his shoulders and said, 'Did he come in?'

It suddenly dawned on me that possibly he hadn't come home at all. I raced downstairs to see if he had slept on the settee but the lounge was cold and empty. I leant against the edge of the door. I just couldn't believe that he was not there, that he would not be there for Christmas. This was going to be another lousy Christmas. Another disaster.

My brother came down and, after greeting my mother, made some fresh tea. Mother was at the sink and I wanted to say something to her about father's absence but was unsure how to raise the subject. She obviously had no intention of mentioning it herself.

'Shall we open a present each, to get into the Christmas spirit?' I asked.

'You two go ahead, I'll wait until later,' she replied.

The two of us decided to wait as well. Feeling dejected and very sad, the morning dragged on as if it would never end. As the smell of the Christmas dinner wafted through the room, I sat staring at the tinsel, twisting and sparkling, and the baubles shining on the tree, and wondered why we'd even bothered. I kept looking out of the window, hoping to see Father coming down the garden path, and when he didn't show I just thought how pointless it all seemed.

As two o'clock approached, Mother decided not to wait for Father to return. I helped dish up four dinners, put three on the table and left one on the side. Though it looked and smelled delicious, we all seemed to have lost our appetites and struggled to eat. Putting a brave face on for Mother's benefit, my brother and I pulled crackers and opened hats, read the mottos and told the jokes. It was all a big charade. Any joy and happiness that might have been enjoyed, through the sharing of a real family Christmas together, was denied to us by my father's usual thoughtless, selfish actions and behaviour. He just didn't care about all the work and effort, the time and care, we had all taken over preparing for Christmas. It made me feel really sad for us all, and very angry with him!

We each had a small piece of Christmas pudding with brandy sauce, this year ignoring tradition and not even bothering to set it aflame. Finally, everything was cleared away and washed up. We sat down and unwrapped presents, constantly aware that we had no idea when, or even if, Father would turn up.

Sitting in the twilight as the fire burned low, we took no notice of the extra luxury items, things we rarely saw the rest of the year, that now surrounded us. Fresh pineapple, figs, dates and tangerines; pretty glass jars with fancy handles that held nuts, chocolates and ginger pieces in a thick syrup; Turkish delight and liqueur chocolates—all lay untouched, ignored. We sat quietly around the hearth, and gazed into the embers of the dying fire, gradually dozing off to sleep.

The noise of the back door opening, and the sound of someone falling inside, brought us all sharply back to life. Someone switched on the Christmas lights, as I prepared to make up the fire. We all knew what was to follow. Father was drunk again. How did he do it? How did he manage to get home? I was so angry with him, I couldn't help wondering why he couldn't just get lost, or better still, arrested. No such luck! He always turned up like the proverbial bad penny. He practically fell into his armchair, as we looked on in disgust. With eyes glazed over, he seemed totally unaware of us all watching him make a spectacle of himself, or even what day it was. He seemed to have no idea of what he had put us all through, or that he'd done anything wrong. Had he been aware, I'm sure he wouldn't have cared anyway. The only positive thing was that he'd returned alone.

We all sat in stunned silence, no one daring to say a word, unsure what his reaction would be. We continued to watch as he laid his head back, eyes rolling, incoherently muttering to himself. This went on for some time before he finally staggered to the bathroom, knocking into furniture and doorways as he went. Mother was both angry and deeply distressed, and didn't seem to know what to do. I suggested that she just ignore him and leave him to sleep off the drink, postponing any discussion or argument until later.

Some considerable time later, Father returned and appeared a little less drunk, having put his head under the tap. His hair was wet, his shirt and collar spattered with water, as were his trousers (though this could have been urine, his aim certain to be more than a bit off given the state he was in!). He seemed to be grinning at us all, with that stupid drunken look of his, and his eyes were bulging. It was a look we had seen time and time again, and was a clear warning to us to expect anything to happen. I hated my father when he was like this. We never knew whether he would overwhelm us with kisses and insincere affection, or if he might loose his temper and act threateningly, or even if he may just try to be nice. Unaware of his strength when he was in such a drunken stupor, he usually ended up hurting someone and either being sorry afterwards or denying the possibility that it could have had anything to do with him.

He managed to shuffle his way back to the armchair, fell untidily into it, and laid his head back, making a weird gurgling noise in his throat as he did so. He lowered his chin and sat staring into the fire. My brother and I decided to go into the sitting room to play cards or a board game, and it wasn't long before Mother joined us. We were quite happy to include her and just pretend Father wasn't even in the house. Mother couldn't concentrate on the game, and we were all on edge as we continually listened for the slightest sound from the living room. It wasn't an easy situation.

As much as we didn't want to go near the living room or disturb Father in any way, we were all in need of a drink and so I volunteered to make some tea. I passed through the living room as quietly as I could, and went rigid when he stirred and changed position in the chair but, thankfully, he didn't wake. I closed the kitchen door and moved as quietly as possible. All the things were on the tray and, as I was about to make my way back, Father awoke. 'Where are you taking that?' he slurred, his voice hardly audible. I told him, and continued to the sitting room. The tea was poured and we all sat quietly, each with his own thoughts, when suddenly the door opened and Father walked in.

Still slurring, and none too friendly, he spoke. 'This is very cosy. I suppose you've all had dinner, so where is mine?'

'In the kitchen on the worktop,' Mother informed him. 'I'll come and get it ready in a minute.'

With that, she finished her tea, picked up the tray and left the room.

Father sat down on the settee and asked what gifts we'd received for Christmas. He acted as if nothing out of the ordinary had taken place, as if we were a normal family having an afternoon tea and chat. I couldn't believe this behaviour, but it was much safer to go along with it than to confront him, so we answered his questions and tried to ignore the fact that he hadn't returned home last night, that he hadn't been there at breakfast, that he hadn't been there to carve the turkey or light the Christmas pudding. That he wasn't there to share in a family Christmas. And the thing that really bugged me, that he hadn't been there to share the joy of feeling, shaking and guessing what was in the gift-wrapped parcels, or the pleasure of unwrapping them. The whole situation just seemed so bizarre. My brother and I knew that he had chosen to stay in the sitting room with us while Mother reheated his dinner, in order to avoid her confronting him. This was yet to come, but she was probably working out the details in her mind at that very moment—what she was going to say and when would be the best time to say it.

Eventually, Mother appeared with a plate of sandwiches and said, 'I am just making some fresh tea. I'll be back in a minute.' When she returned the tea tray was laden with sandwiches, cakes and mince pies. As she put the tray down, she told Father his dinner was on the table. 'We'll have our tea in here,' she added. 'If you kids want any pickles or anything else, you'll have to get them yourselves.'

This was a clear act of defiance, since she knew that Father would expect all of us to sit at the dining table together, regardless of what we were eating. It was another of his strict rules, that we all ate together. Much to our surprise, he made no comment, left the room and shut the door, obviously deciding against making a stand at this time. We gave a sigh of relief that, for the time being, we would not have to sit through another hostile atmosphere or major row.

Mother poured the tea and my brother and I ate most of the sandwiches and cake (Mother still seemed to have no appetite). Normally Father would have rather ceremoniously sliced the ham, but today Mother had done everything. She was obviously very unhappy and bottling up her emotions. I don't know if I was expected to comment but, after she had been sitting quietly for a while, she began to voice her feelings.

'How dare he? What a nerve your father has. Spends all night with his whore, comes home drunk, demands his food and just thinks he is going to carry on as if nothing has happened. That is not going to happen. He has ruined yet another Christmas, but I'll make sure it doesn't happen again. I am not planning any more Christmases, or preparing for them. I'll make arrangements for us to go away next year, or to spend Christmas with someone else.'

Mother's calmness surprised me but I felt sure that she was anything but calm inside. She looked deflated, defeated and utterly miserable. Their marriage had always been fiery in nature, and I wondered what the coming days were to bring for us all.

# CHAPTER 9
## The Confrontation

I don't remember much about the rest of that Christmas Day. Presumably it was fairly uneventful since I'm sure I would recall any further incidents.

On Boxing Day I suppose I must have done my paper round, though I don't recall that either. However, the day seemed to have started when we all went to a friend's house for a buffet and drinks, which had become usual practice now that Father and his partner, Mr Gray, were doing a lot of work, and Mother was friendly with Mrs Gray. My brother and I were friends of their son, and they also had a daughter (who was quite a bit older than us) but she was at her boyfriend's for the day.

Mr and Mrs Gray were a lovely couple, who always made us feel welcome. She was a big, jolly lady with loads of energy, who knew exactly what to provide to keep everyone happy. Great with teenagers as well as younger children, she had an incredible amount of patience. Mr Gray was a stocky, quiet but cheerful soul, with a strong country accent that seemed to suit him. He reminded me of a jolly, fat farmer, as he always had a ruddy face and usually wore a flat cap. However, this particular day he wore no cap and it seemed strange to see his shiny, bald head poking out of his horseshoe of grey hair just above his ears.

We children were sent off to play in the children's room, leaving the adults to talk. Kevin (the son) had all the latest toys as well as lots of grown-up things that we didn't have and he was very happy to let us share his things. He had a Scalextric track set around the edge of the room, intertwined with an electric train set, and this was often played with by the adults too. He had his own record player, tape recorder and radio. On the snooker table lay a pile of records in an untidy heap, which included all the latest hits, of which we sorted out eight to put on the automatic record player.

Later on we all enjoyed Mrs Gray's buffet-style lunch, consisting of lots of meats with pickles and chutneys, and leftovers from Christmas made into hot bubble-and-squeak cakes. There were flans, tarts, sausage rolls and mince pies, as well as several different types of cake. A bowl of fruit punch was provided for us children and a variety of drinks on a bar for the adults. Mrs Gray was a great cook and wanted everyone to try a piece of everything so you always came away feeling really stuffed. It was a very happy environment, even though my parents made sure they steered clear of each other. If anyone noticed, they never said anything. It was such a pleasant day and seemed to run on into the evening, with empty plates continuously being re-stocked. When it was time to go home, we were all reluctant to leave. Kisses and hugs were exchanged, the goodbyes said, and we then walked the short distance home.

Mother looked worn and tired, the strain of the last two days having taken its toll. Father seemed to be his usual perky, lively self. Once inside the house, Mother checked and stoked the fire whilst my brother and I headed for the sitting room in case there was a row looming. There was. What provoked the argument that then erupted we had no idea, but the explosion of abuse that followed left my brother and me with our mouths open, aghast at the language Mother was throwing at Father. We sat rooted to the spot, not daring to move, but very thankful that we weren't in the same room. The yelling and screaming was so loud we could hear every word.

'Don't you dare think you can carry on in this house as if nothing has happened. Keep your filthy hands off me. How dare you bring your latest whore into our home and expect me to entertain her! You have gone too far this time and I've had enough,' screamed Mother.

'Mai Ling is not a whore,' Father replied. 'She is a nurse at the hospital and just a friend who is on her own at Christmas.'

'A nurse she may be, but more than a friend to you. You must think I'm stupid, to think that you haven't been sharing her bed, and knowing you, it has probably been going on for ages,' Mother retorted. 'What sort of example do you think you are setting your children? How do you expect them to show you any respect? They aren't babies any more.'

She paused for breath and carried on, 'I don't suppose you are the only one either. Don't flatter yourself. She has her own quarters and there are plenty of men around. You are probably one of many.'

We heard the smack. It was usually the back of his hand, and we knew from experience how much that hurt. The ensuing silence was deafening.

Mother had obviously picked up the dish bought as a present by Mai Ling, and thrown it at my father. 'I don't want any reminders of your women in my home,' she yelled. 'Just as well she didn't come for Christmas lunch or I would have tipped it all over her.'

The dish must have been made of a very robust material, certainly not plastic, for it didn't crack, break or even chip. It looked like glass but was seemingly indestructible: Mother picked it up and smashed it onto the iron bar round the hearth, but venting her anger on it had no effect. Mother began screaming and crashing the dish against anything in a bid to destroy it, whilst Father poured forth a torrent of foul, abusive language, in between calling her a 'bitch' and a 'cow'. She managed to stay just beyond his reach as he attempted to grab her arms and hit her.

My brother and I sat looking at each other, frightened of doing nothing yet too terrified to get involved. There was a crash and the sound of breaking glass. The verbal abuse became drowned out by the sound of chairs and other items being knocked and scraped across the floor. The yelling and shouting became less distinct as they gasped for breath through the fighting. The level of noise was such that we imagined the whole street could hear. The old lady next door was almost deaf but I still hoped that she was still away with her family for the holiday.

The fighting and screaming, thumping and scraping, seemed to go on for ever. I looked at my brother and asked him what I should do, whether I should try and get help. 'Should I run to the telephone box and ring the police?'

He looked at me with big frightened eyes and said, 'Would anyone come? If they did, what then?'

We stuck it out. Things did seem to have quietened down. Father slammed out of the room and pounded upstairs. We heard a door crash, and then the thump of his footfalls as he paced up and down in the bedroom overhead. I quickly slipped across the hall and peered round the living room door. Amongst the destruction lay my mother on a chair, her arm over her head, hair and clothes in disarray, with tears streaming down her face. The Christmas tree lay sprawled on its side, its shiny baubles now broken and scattered around the floor along with upturned furniture, broken picture frames and smashed glass.

The Chinese dish lay upturned in the middle of it all, still in one piece, despite the attempts to destroy it.

It seemed the Season of Goodwill was over for us, if indeed it had ever arrived at all. The New Year approached, and we had no good memories to take with us. Although the dish did finally get broken, the memories could not be erased and Mai Ling stayed on the scene for some time. There were threats of divorce, and there were weekends when my father stayed out, but Mother stood her ground, refusing to give way.

Eventually, Mai Ling met a doctor and moved away from the area but by then the damage had taken its toll and Mother suffered a nervous breakdown. She finally gathered enough courage to visit the doctor to tell him why she was so depressed and falling apart. The doctor was a family friend who knew all about my father's lifestyle. He suggested to Mother that she play Father at his own game and find herself another man! My mother lost her temper at this point and told him in no uncertain terms what she thought of his suggestion. She told him to 'go to hell', and declared that she would not cheapen herself by sinking to my father's level. Mother made her feelings quite clear to him, saying, 'I'm not interested in lowering my own moral standards. That won't solve anything. I refuse to behave like a whore to ease his guilty conscience. I'm amazed, and disgusted, that you would suggest such a thing.'

Picking up her things, she turned to the doctor and said, 'I can't believe you've just made such a suggestion to me. You, with your deeply religious Roman Catholic views, should have much higher standards. I find your suggestion insulting.'

She walked away from the surgery in tears. The friendship with the family doctor was severed and it was a partner at the same practice that helped my mother through her breakdown.

The arguments and tension at home got worse. Mother would often taunt my father and, at every opportunity, would bring up the past and throw it in his face. The two of them tried reconciliation but Mother couldn't put the past behind her. Things just went from bad to worse.

# Chapter **10**
## Accusations and Lies

For a period of time the rows at home affected my schoolwork, and I was accused of not trying or of wasting my education. Following a really bad school report, my father told me to pull my socks up or there would be no going out, I'd be kept in. In addition, piano practice was suffering and I'd failed one of my piano exams. Early on I had done really well, reaching Grade 5 by the time I was thirteen years old. But, as I practised less and less, I was told I was wasting hard earned money and being selfish, so—the piano was sold!

I made a determined effort to knuckle down and make a real effort, to prove to myself and my teachers that I was at least as good as they expected me to be. I really studied hard, did enormous amounts of homework, and made sure it was always handed in on time. Such a vast improvement did I make that, at the end of term, I came top of the class. The teachers invited my parents to discuss my future but Father refused to attend. My father had very strong, fixed ideas about what I should do on leaving school, and we often had disagreements about the matter. He wanted me to take up hairdressing or become a telephonist, neither of which I wanted to do. Adamant that I would be leaving school at the earliest possible opportunity in order to earn my keep, my father had no interest in further education for me nor in my having a career. So, I was denied the opportunity of going to college with several of my friends, and staying on at school for a further year was out of the question.

The school had hoped to change his mind about my leaving and neither the teachers nor the headmistress could understand his attitude. Miss Smitham was both angry and distressed and, even though letters were sent home and phone calls made, nothing anyone said could dissuade him or make any difference.

Even so, in my last year of school I worked hard preparing for exams, and still looked forward to a chance of further education. The form mistress was a Mrs Prior, a very strict but lovely teacher, whom we all respected. She had great faith in me and was sure I would do well. However, during the Christmas term all the classes were brought together to rehearse for the Christmas play, a grand affair usually, that attracted large audiences. In one of the other classes was an awful female called Jasmine, a nasty bully who ridiculed and fought with others, and bragged about her experiences and (s)exploits with the opposite sex. I didn't like her one bit. One afternoon I was in the washrooms near the gym when Jasmine and three of her cronies came in, discussing men, sex and experiences, loudly enough for all to hear. On seeing me, she stood directly behind me, looked past me into the mirror, fluffed her hair and began to laugh.

'Your father is a good screw, very experienced. Knows all the right buttons to press. I've learned a lot from him,' she said, staring at my reflection.

I rounded on her and spat, 'My father wouldn't be interested in you.'

She threw her head back and shrieked with laughter saying, 'That's where you're wrong. We spent three hours in bed together the other night and he did things to me you just wouldn't believe.'

I was so shocked I was finding this hard to take in. My mind was racing and I thought, surely my father wouldn't go to bed with a schoolgirl. And what does he see in her anyway?

I called her a liar and she looked at me as she began moving her body, running her hands over her breasts, down over her stomach and between her legs. Her friends lay back against the tiled wall sniggering and smirking.

'He could do things to me that no one ever has. He made me orgasm, he kissed me between my legs and licked and sucked me until I was begging him to stop. No more boys for me. It's real men from now on and I can't wait to get your father into bed again.'

My stomach churned.

She carried on, 'You don't even know what it's like with a boy. You don't know what you're missing.'

She came towards me, poking me in the chest with her forefinger, while her friends looked on. I backed away until I had finally heard enough. It was as if I exploded. I hit her finger away and she caught my wrist. We started fighting, the bystanders cheering and shouting as she grabbed my hair and yanked my head back. I did the same to her. We were kicking and punching, and somehow I found myself pushed back into one of the toilet cubicles. We were both on the floor by this time and, without hesitation, I pushed her head into the toilet pan and flushed it, holding her head down with all my strength, whilst I sat astride on her back.

Suddenly, a deep, booming voice brought the riot to a halt. Mrs Prior stood red-faced, hands on hips, and yelled, 'Just what is going on here? Ingrid, you should know better, and Jasmine— I might have guessed you'd be involved!' She glared at us both and, pointing to the door, said, 'Headmistress's office, immediately!' The onlookers all slunk away and disappeared quietly. Jasmine and I walked across the main hall and waited in the corridor in stony silence. Staring at the sign on the door, 'M. Smitham – Headmistress', we ignored each other and waited.

Mrs Prior swept up the corridor, knocked on the door and swiftly entered when a voice from beyond called 'come in'. The sounds of muffled conversation could be heard before the door opened and we were ordered to go in. Mrs Prior stood holding the door open as we entered and she looked at me with a hurt and angry expression. Standing in front of the large, heavy oak desk, we watched as the headmistress continued writing on some papers in front of her. Finally, she calmly put down her pen, looked up and rose to stand with her back to the window. Over her shoulder I could see the school groundsman working in the rosebeds, his wheelbarrow alongside and various garden implements lying on the path.

Miss Smitham looked us both up and down before she spoke. 'Well, Ingrid. I am surprised at you. You have disgraced yourself!' Holding out her hand, she added, 'I will take the Prefect badge. You are no longer worthy of the position you hold in this school.'

Turning to Jasmine, she said, 'In your case, Jasmine, I suppose I can expect nothing better. You don't need to look for trouble, it usually finds you.' She continued, 'You should both be ashamed of your behaviour, behaving like a couple of alley cats. You are supposed to be here, learning to behave like young ladies.'

She walked around the desk, her hands behind her back, and muttered something inaudible to Mrs Prior, who still stood near the door. Miss Smitham returned to sit behind her desk, as we both stood looking straight ahead in defiance. I was feeling anxious, waiting for the next development.

'What brought on this disgraceful behaviour?' she asked. When she received no response from either of us she asked, 'Have either of you anything to say?'

Silence. We both jumped as her tone changed and she bellowed across the desk. 'Look at me when I am speaking to you. Ingrid, what have you got to say for yourself?'

I looked at her and said, 'Nothing Miss Smitham.' She turned and asked the same question of Jasmine who replied, 'Nothing Miss.'

Miss Smitham then banged the desk with her hand, making us

both jump. She yelled, 'Nothing, Miss Smitham? Right,' said Miss Smitham, 'for fighting in the gym locker room toilets, there is a penalty of two strokes. You will both get one week's detention, and I will be writing to your parents.'

She approached the glass cabinet at the side of her desk and removed the willow stick. Still glaring straight ahead, my stomach churned but I was determined not to show how afraid I was. Miss Smitham went back to her desk. 'Right, hold out your left hands,' she said.

Both of us obeyed the instruction. With precision the cane whooshed twice through the air and, with a resounding crack, made contact with bare flesh. The excruciating pain as the wood cut across the palm forced Jasmine to back away biting her lip, but I stood my ground. As the second stroke fell, I flinched and tears sprang to my eyes.

The headmistress returned the cane to the cupboard, saying over her shoulder, 'I hope that teaches you both a lesson. I don't want to see either of you in here again. In detention you will write a hundred lines: "I must not fight with other pupils and must set an example to the rest of the school." You are dismissed.'

We both left the room with our heads up, defiant, determined and still ignoring each other. My hand was stinging and painful so I went straight to the toilets to run it under cold water, and burst into tears. Being left-handed meant I would have a few problems, not to mention the one I would have explaining to my parents that I was no longer a prefect.

For the rest of the day, my hand throbbed and I had great difficulty in writing. As the school day came to a close, Jasmine and I were sent to a classroom where we began to write out a hundred lines. Needless to say, we sat as far from each other as possible. The teacher overseeing our detention marked books and said nothing until an hour later when it was time to pack up our things and go home.

I cycled the three miles home, with a heavy satchel strapped to my back. When I arrived Mother asked me why I was so late.

'Oh, I had some work to do in the library,' I lied.

I thought I might be able to get away with saying nothing but my parents noticed that I couldn't hold a fork properly whilst eating, and that I was having difficulty in using a pen. Mother asked what I had done to my hand. My stomach churned and, in front of my parents and my brother, I admitted that I had got the cane at school. An interrogation followed as they inspected my hand, the red weal still painfully evident across the palm. I had to explain what had happened, how we were fighting and then frog-marched to the headmistress's office, how I lost my prefect status and the detention.

When my father asked what I had been fighting for, I told him that Jasmine had been talking and laughing about me with her friends. As realisation dawned on him that he knew the person I was talking about, he became edgy and immediately finished questioning me.

He said, 'Right young lady, you can get ready for bed, take your homework up with you and I'll be up in a minute.'

I knew from experience what would follow from this so, fearfully and in trepidation, I went to my bedroom and paced the floor as I awaited a further good hiding. I heard my father's tread on the stairs and watched the door handle, waiting for it to turn. I looked into his face as he stood in the doorway. I was frightened but I was also stubborn. I knew what to expect but this time I had some ammunition of my own. Would I be brave enough to use it? Would I be able to throw it in his face? I had to consider my mother who was sitting in the room below, and who could hear what was taking place. I decided it was best to say nothing, take the beating, and save the ammunition for some other time.

That night I slept fitfully, if I slept at all. I now had weals across my backside and the tops of my legs, to go with the pain and discomfort in my hand. 'It was certainly difficult being a child,' I thought.

In the following March I was sixteen. My school report read, 'Why has Ingrid no ambition?' The reason was, I didn't want to stay on at school anymore, and I didn't want to study. I'd lost all interest. Father was to get his own way after all, though for a very different reason.

# Chapter 11
## My Living Nightmare

Weathered by my life experiences, and now in middle age, I look back and still shudder and cry about the time that was to change my whole life for ever. Will I ever forget that night? It was horrendous, and I still bear the scars. I just can't believe the way events unfolded, and never thought I would ever be able to write about them.

I was fifteen years old. My father and I had been working all day in a hotel lounge. The large room was filled with furniture covered in dustsheets and all moved into the centre of the room. Two single beds had been left for us to sleep on so that we could work for as long as possible into the night, in order to finish in the shortest possible time before the Christmas rush began. The busy hoteliers were taking advantage of a slack period for bookings, to have work carried out with the minimum of disruption to their growing business.

I had been stripping wallpaper and my father had been preparing the paintwork ready for repainting. In the late afternoon he left and went out drinking, leaving me behind to carry on stripping paper. We were supposed to be finishing this room, or the preparation of it at least, but when he returned, late in the evening, he was very drunk. I'd been here before, but tonight there was something very different about him. As he came into the room, bringing some sandwiches and a drink for me, he had a glazed look in his eyes. This was not unusual, but the dark evil look of his penetrating stare was new to me, and I was filled with a strange, overwhelming fear and dread. I wasn't sure why I felt this way. This was my father, dammit, so why should I be scared of this man?

While we were eating our sandwiches, my father got around to the subject of boyfriends. He wanted to know what boyfriends I'd had, how far they had been with me, what we had got up to. Had we just kissed and fondled or had it gone beyond that to petting? How far had I been prepared to go with them? I didn't want to answer his questions. I thought this was personal and, as a fifteen-year-old who had never discussed sex with her father before, I just wasn't comfortable talking about it. My mother had taught me the facts of life, and sex education at school filled in the rest but, as for being prepared, and the down to earth discussion on how to prevent unwanted pregnancy, I'm afraid most girls discovered these things too late.

Father seemed to delight in making me feel uncomfortable, and pressed me to tell him just how much I knew. I was naïve, and not very well informed, and when he started to discuss the delights and pleasures of orgasm, I didn't know what he was talking about.

Father went out to the bathroom and I began clearing things away. After a short while, he came back into the room. I was facing him, and the look in his eyes terrified me. For the first time in my life I knew real fear and I shivered. He had a look of evil, and he glared at me. This wasn't the father I knew. I was afraid and, as I was backing away from him, almost stumbled over the side of one of the beds, I was cold with fear, but my palms were hot and sweaty, and I pressed myself against the wall. Father kept coming towards me and I realised he hadn't pulled up the zip on his trousers. I couldn't take my eyes off his face. I tried to stay calm. I said to him, 'What's the matter, what's wrong?'

His reply was, 'You are the matter—that's what's wrong. You're growing up to be a beautiful woman, and I'm jealous of your freedom and your boyfriends.' I was shocked at this. My father was jealous of my boyfriends? He was twenty-one years older than me, for Christ's sake.

My mind was racing. I was looking for a means of escape. Weird thoughts ran through my brain as I tried to bluff my way out of the situation.

I was slowly feeling my way along the wall to get as far away from him as I could, and looking for any means of escape. As he continued towards me, I just didn't know what to do. I was backed into a corner against the wall. He came forward, undoing his trousers, and by this the time I was petrified.

He got nearer and he said, 'I'm going to have you before anyone else does.'

I was flat against the wall, saying, 'Dad, what are you doing?'

My voice was shaking, I was trembling. He flattened me against the wall and started kissing me. He started rubbing his hands all over my body, and I went frigid, unable to move. This man slobbering all over me was my father. I couldn't believe what was happening to me. He ran his hands down my sides, and then he loosened my trousers. I was trying to hang on and, with tears running down my face, trying to fight him off, but he lost his temper and threw me onto one of the beds.

The shock gave me a jolt and I attempted to get up, thinking I could run for the door, but as I did so, he pushed me back down, tearing at my clothes. I felt completely helpless and the more I struggled, the worse it seemed. My trousers were somewhere down around my ankles and I was finding it difficult to move. Breathing became difficult and I was gasping for air. I always used to wonder how women got raped. I couldn't understand how a man could get your clothes off and rape you if you'd got two hands and you were fighting back. Now, I found myself on the bed, with my arms pinned up above my head. I remember the pain and the burning sensation as he entered me. My body felt as if it was on fire, as my father continued driving into me. I realised then that a man intent on rape can find superhuman strength. I couldn't do anything to stop him. I was terrified, petrified, and unable to move. Who was this man? My father? No! This was more like the devil. This was evil! I didn't know this man. This was a stranger. I stared, horrified, at the face of this changed personality, this person I didn't know, and I wanted to scream. But no sound would come from my mouth. I seemed to have no control over any of my senses, and my head was thumping.

I gasped out that I was going to scream if he didn't stop, but he put his hand over my mouth and held me down, still driving into me, saying, 'I'm going to be the first, nobody else is going to deflower you. I'm going to be the first.'

His body was heavy, and he was hurting me. The pain—the searing pain—the agony. It was excruciating, as if my insides were being ripped out, as if I was being ripped apart and torn to shreds.

He was heavy and stank of booze. He was hateful, and slobbering all over me, and I loathed it. He was kissing my breasts and biting me, his face rough and unshaven, and it seemed to go on and on for such a long time. I felt as if I was going to black out. I struggled to stay aware, willing myself to stay conscious. Somehow I knew I had to stay awake. He seemed to be exhausted, and collapsed on top of me and then rolled over onto his side.

I don't remember him leaving. I just remember lying there, curled up, feeling disgusting, filthy, sick, ashamed. Curling up tightly into a ball and just lying there, I wept and I wept and I wept. I must have slept for a while. When I awoke, I thought at first that I'd been having a nightmare. I felt sticky between my legs, I felt unclean and uncomfortable. It took me a while to realise where I was, and the pain throughout my body made me aware that this was no bad dream. I just wanted to get into a bath. I lay there for what seemed like hours, unable to think straight, not knowing what to do. I sat on the side of the bed, my head and arms hanging between my legs. I felt sick and my body retched. How could I ever face my father again? He'd just raped me.

I sat there, just looking round the room, the discoloured, patchy walls glaring back at me. I remember thinking that this would be the last time I would ever do any work to help my father. I just didn't know what to do next. My body was sore and burning, and it felt as if I'd been beaten up. I got up from the bed and looked down to find my thighs covered in blood and semen. I was so frightened. I didn't know whether I should tell anyone, or what to do. I felt so sick with shame and disgust that I was retching. I cleaned myself up as best I could and pulled my clothes on. I felt a wreck, dejected, miserable. It was difficult to walk, or even stand upright, as I groped my way to the door. The cold, fresh air swept over me. I gasped, and welcomed the outdoors.

I don't remember how I got home, but as soon as I got there I ran a hot bath and sat in it. I had scratches around my breasts and thighs, and the hot water made my skin sting. I just wanted to scrub myself clean but it just made things worse. My body was red and raw, scratched and sore, and I just wanted to crawl into a hole and hide away. I felt disgusting and there was no one I felt I could talk to.

I avoided my father because I didn't know how to face him and I knew that my mother would pick up on an atmosphere. Somehow, I didn't see him for a while, I kept out of his way. We both avoided each other. I was terrified of ever turning up at home with him being there on his own. I didn't know how to broach the subject, I didn't know what to say, and I didn't like being alone with him. I wore clothes that covered me completely, roll-neck jumpers and trousers. I didn't undress until I was alone in my room. And, I was terrified that I could be pregnant. Though the scratches slowly faded, the scars were to haunt me for years to come.

That Christmas I announced that I was going to stay with my grandparents. I didn't ask permission, I just made a very determined statement of intention. Mother looked at Father to check his response to this but, as none was forthcoming, there were no comments or objections.

# CHAPTER **12**
## New Horizons

I was sixteen in the March, and had been rebelling about all sorts of things. I was leaving school to go to work. I had pestered my mother to let me join a youth club and was allowed to do so on the condition that I would walk to the club with friends and Father would collect me at 10.00 pm. This was embarrassing but it was a start. The rape incident was never, ever mentioned. In fact, he acted as if it had never happened. He just seemed to shut his mind to the whole incident.

The youth club was in the centre of town, which at night was a far cry from the bustling shopping centre of the daytime. Entrance to the club was through a door in a side street and the club itself was situated on the first floor of the building. There was a coffee bar area, a sitting room with lounging chairs and sofas, and a small dance floor.

I had been going to the club for a while and had made a lot of new friends, in particular an ex-convent girl called Lynn,[1] who'd led a very sheltered existence and was now branching out. Lynn was very beautiful. She was blue-eyed, had lovely, natural strawberry-blonde hair, and her very pale skin was lightly freckled. Tall and willowy, she certainly turned heads, but males seemed to be a bit afraid of her, though I didn't exactly know why. She had just had a portfolio of photographs put together, in preparation for a career in modelling, and had been travelling backwards and forwards to London to

---

1    Name has been changed to protect identity

photographic sessions at several different studios and locations.

It was at the club that I also met Eric.[2] Tall and good looking, he came from a village seven miles out of town and worked as a panel beater at a local garage. When we danced together it seemed as if we had been doing it all our lives, and when he kissed me for the first time, I almost collapsed with fright. I couldn't believe this guy could like me. We started dating and he met my parents who, fortunately, knew him since his parents and mine had all gone to school together. Another bonus was that Eric had his own car and could bring me home from the youth club.

We began to go out on trips at the weekend. We would go tenpin bowling, or take walks along the river, perhaps go boating or to the coast. For my birthday I was taken out to dinner and then shopping for clothes. We were in love and inseparable. My parents seemed to be pleased and we were trusted to be out and about or left alone without too much interference.

That year, I was invited to spend Christmas with his family, who I had come to know and found very friendly and welcoming. It was a fun time, in that lovely, cosy house. Eric's brother and his fiancée were also there and we ate and drank, opened our presents, and then played cards and games like charades and pass the parcel. It was the best Christmas I could remember. On Boxing Day we visited my grandparents, who also knew Eric and his family, and they were very pleased for me.

I slept over at Eric's, in his bed, while Eric and his brother slept downstairs in the lounge. In the morning, Eric brought me a cup of tea in bed and we sat and chatted. The chat turned to kissing and then to petting, until I felt things were going too far and I got scared. Thankfully, Eric accepted the limits I set and, instead, asked me what I thought about getting engaged! I couldn't believe it. I was shocked. It became clear that he was serious and so we sealed the

---

2    Name has been changed to protect identity

occasion with a kiss and some breast fondling!

We got engaged on my seventeenth birthday and initially planned to save for a couple of years before arranging a wedding. Everyone was over the moon—my family, his family, my grandparents and his—and things were suddenly wonderful.

That summer was a dream, although there were odd times when things got difficult. Passion would run riot and we'd get into heavy petting sessions, at which point I would freeze. At first Eric let it go and didn't say anything but, as time went on, he began to feel that I was never going to let our relationship blossom and accused me of being frigid. I told him that nothing would happen until I was married.

Lynn and her boyfriend often made up a foursome and we would all go either to the local dance, the pub or for picnics in nearby Hatfield Forest. When Lynn's romance ended she came to me for a shoulder to cry on and I was the one who helped her over the worst. Eric was very supportive, every inch a gentleman and, if she visited during the evening, he would always drop her off on his way home.

Was I blind or just foolish, or was I so in love with Eric that I could never see any wrong in him? We had been out buying Christmas presents and met Lynn. We decided to go for a coffee and at the local café we chatted and laughed. I noticed the touchy-feely laughing and the sideways glances between Lynn and Eric but ignored it. However, one evening Eric arrived late and flustered and, without putting his arms around me, he gave me a quick peck on the cheek instead of the long passionate kiss I had got used to. I was quite taken aback and asked him if something was wrong. I could see from his expression that things were definitely not right.

He took a deep breath and said, 'I want to talk to you about taking a break for a while.'

Casually, I asked, 'What sort of break, a holiday? A weekend away?'

'No! Not that sort of break. I mean, not to see each other for a while.'

I was suddenly feeling queasy. With butterflies in my stomach, I tried to put on a brave front. I said, 'You mean, the engagement's off. You want your ring back?'

'Something like that,' he replied. 'I don't want the ring back. I just want some breathing space.'

I asked him if there was someone else, whether it was something I'd said or done, or whether it was something deeper, like not letting him have sex.

'It's all and none of them,' he said. 'I don't want to hurt you, I love you.'

'Do you, Eric?' I asked. 'I don't believe you could possibly love me if that is what you want.' I felt cold and hurt and badly let down. I wanted to cry but I was not going to let him see me in tears. 'Ok Eric, if that's the way you feel. I want you to go now. I will think about the ring, and if you feel the same way in a month's time, we'll talk about it.'

He picked his jacket up from the back of the chair and, turning to walk away, he said, 'I'll see you soon. Good night.'

I sat down on the couch. I was stunned. As I stared down at my beautiful engagement ring the tears streamed down my face. I wished I could have just died. My mother came into the room, commenting on Eric's short visit and wanting to know if something was wrong? I looked up, the tears just flowing, and raced to the hall door and upstairs to my bedroom, where I threw myself onto the bed and just sobbed.

I didn't see Eric for over two weeks. I didn't feel I could go to the places we usually went to, and rumours that we had split up were soon rife. Friends stopped me to enquire whether the engagement was off. I told them we were just having a cooling-off period, although I don't think I believed it myself.

And then I saw them. Arm in arm, laughing and kissing. Oh, did it hurt. I was still madly in love with him. We'd been going out together for nine months and by then had planned to marry the following June, but Lynn made sure that we were never to get that far. I found her draped over Eric one night at the youth club, my best friend. He told me the engagement was off, and that he and Lynn were going out together. A beautiful friendship then ended. I'd lost my fiancé and my best friend, all in the space of one evening.

My heart ached. My head was swimming and I felt sick to the bottom of my stomach. The thought of him and Lynn had never occurred to me—and yet here they were, my fiancé and my best friend. I had been too blind to see it before. I went home, feeling low and dejected. I took off the engagement ring and, with a heavy, aching heart, put it back in the box and began to write:

> My darling Eric,
> Today I saw you and Lynn together, my ex-fiancé and my so-called good friend. She may be glamorous and sexy. She may wear expensive clothes and shoes, and she may let you go all the way, but she will never love you the way I do.
>
> I had thought of selling the ring and keeping the money for 'breach of promise' but perhaps it would look better on Lynn, although she may want something bigger, better and far more expensive.
>
> I love you very much, but I know it is no good if it is one-sided so, although I am very upset, I can only wish you well and hope that we may remain friends. I can't say the same of Lynn.
> Love,
> Ingrid

The next few weeks were dismal and depressing. I couldn't keep my mind on anything and finally, after a really awful week at work,

I ended it by having a disagreement with my supervisor. I walked out that night in a raging temper and phoned in sick the next day. I went to the station, bought a ticket to Liverpool Street station and went to London in search of a job.

I registered with an employment agency and, after completing tests for typing, English and maths, was immediately given the opportunity of an interview for a position at a large Eastern bank. Armed with directions, I headed for the city. This was my first visit and I was completely overawed by the size of the buildings and the busy streets. This was a whole new world and I found it all very exciting.

I moved through the big, heavy revolving doorway and was greeted by the commissionaire, who directed me to the Personnel Department. The banking hall was cavernous. Approximately fifty people worked behind counters, desks and glass panels, and there was a lot of to-ing and fro-ing. Young lads in dark, gold-braided uniforms and pillbox hats mingled with similarly dressed gentleman who wore top hats.

I mounted the wide stone staircase, in the centre of which more uniformed men operated lifts. Everything seemed so well organised and ran like clockwork. I knocked on the door labelled 'Personnel Department' and entered. In the large, airy room a typist sat speaking on the phone, behind an enormous desk covered with papers and forms. Trays stacked to the side announced 'In', 'Out' and 'Pending'. This was all a far cry from the small dismal places I had worked.

As the young lady replaced the handset, she confirmed my name with me and offered me a seat, explaining that the Personnel Officer would see me shortly. I was completely bowled over by her offer of tea or coffee and politely accepted the latter. She disappeared through a door behind her and, within a very short space of time, returned with two steaming cups and offered the sugar and milk as she handed a cup to me.

I was then given an application form and asked to complete it in my own time. As I sat on the large, comfortable settee, I thought to myself, 'This office is better furnished than our lounge.' Everything seemed so fresh and big and new to me. I handed the completed form to the typist, who quickly glanced through it, and, saying she wouldn't be a moment, she took the form into a room marked 'Personnel Manager'. The heavy oak door opened again from which emerged a very elegantly dressed, older lady. With very dark hair and a swarthy skin, she was well made up and dripping with gold jewellery, chains, pendants, earrings, brooches, a watch and even an ankle chain. I always thought ankle chains identified a prostitute. Well, how wrong could I get?

Hand outstretched, the lady came forward and introduced herself, and invited me into her large, modern office. We chatted about my present job and the reason for my wishing to work in the city. She then told me about a position in the Securities Department, working with stocks and shares certificates. A very pleasant gentleman, who could have easily doubled for Adolf Hitler, was to take me to meet the department manager who would show me the ropes.

I followed him up a marble staircase to the first floor, and into an equally large open plan office where a lady was using a clamp-like machine to open heavy folders, which were in turn clamped between thick leather cases. These held the sheets on which clients' stocks and shares were recorded and then logged. The certificates themselves were piled up and sent to the vault each evening. The whole work floor was a hive of activity, with a continual buzz of conversation, phones constantly ringing and people carrying files and papers quickly moving to and fro.

By the time I had been introduced to ladies I would be working with, the section supervisor, the secretaries and one or two other people, my head was spinning and I couldn't remember anyone's name. 'Hitler' and I seemed to get on fine, and by the end of the interview I had secured a position at The Chartered Bank. As it was lunchtime I was offered a luncheon voucher that I could use at a nearby restaurant, and an envelope to return to the employment agency.

I was more excited than hungry so after a snack lunch I returned to the agency. I was warmly greeted and congratulated by the girls there.

'You can now join the city set,' they said.

The bank had already been in touch with the agency, a start date agreed and the salary was to be £1,000 per annum. Apparently, the bank had sounded very pleased about me. After handing over the envelope, I was asked to sign a certificate of acceptance, and a notice to confirm the agreed salary. With a handshake and a cheerful goodbye, I left the agency floating on air.

As I walked along the streets I had a chance to study the surrounding area, noticing the cavernous glass dome of Liverpool Street station, and how vast and busy the station actually was. Passing the inspector on the platform, I opened the nearest carriage door and sank into a seat on the 2.15 pm train to Cambridge. Mulling over the events of the day, I felt really pleased with myself. A new confidence was building inside me. I felt happy and more contented than I had been in a very long time.

I walked the mile from the station, arriving home before anyone else. I made myself a cup of tea and went upstairs to my room. I took out my writing case and wrote a letter of resignation to the Harlow Development Corporation (where I currently worked). I wondered how my parents would react to my news. I felt that I had really achieved something and felt proud. It seemed suddenly that no one could dampen my spirits. I no longer felt that familiar pang of hurt when I thought about Eric. I thought to myself that I was now going up in the world and I would show them all.

I went downstairs and laid the table for dinner, turned on the radio and read the newspaper. I was so full of confidence that I felt no fear in telling my parents, or of handing in my notice, or indeed any qualms about having told the office I was sick. I just felt deeply contented and decided that this was where my life would begin to change. I was about to make my mark!

The change in job also meant a change in friends and a change of social life. I started going to dances in London, and was generally enjoying life and having a good time. However, one morning as I stepped off the train at Liverpool Street, a familiar figure alighted from the carriage ahead of mine. Lynn looked her usual glamorous self and, as we passed through the barrier, she turned and caught sight of me.

Guardedly, she said, 'Hello, how are you?'

'Fine,' I replied, 'and you?'

'Oh, I'm ok,' she said. 'Actually, I'm glad I've seen you. I'm off to France to a fashion show this week and it looks as though I may be travelling around the world for three months with my job.'

It was on the tip of my tongue to ask after Eric but I decided against it. We parted company, she to the underground and I to the city streets.

Two or three weeks passed and then one evening, as I walked home from the station, a car pulled alongside me and a familiar voice asked, 'Can I give you a lift?'

As realisation hit me, I went weak at the knees and my stomach somersaulted. I casually opened the door and got in the car, as if I had no control over my actions at all.

We made small talk for a while, until we reached my garden gate. Eric then turned to me and said, 'Can I take you to the dance on Saturday?' I was so surprised, I said I wasn't sure if I was free.

With a hurt look on his face he said, 'I know you are not going out with anyone else, and Lynn and I have finished.'

I told him I would think about it and, as I got out of the car and shut the door firmly, I decided I would not be used in that way. I turned to give a slight wave and then went indoors.

My mind was in turmoil. I considered the options: see Eric again; tell him to get lost; go out with him to string him along and then dump him, like he did me, to get my revenge. As Saturday night approached, I'd made my decision and, when the phone rang on Friday evening, I answered it, knowing that it was Eric calling to ask if I was going to the dance. I told him I was and, since I'd already decided what I was going to do, agreed he could call for me at eight o'clock.

With butterflies in my stomach but determined to see my plan through, I put on my make-up and dancing shoes, and got ready for the dance. A keen but over-anxious Eric arrived well before eight o'clock but I took my time, practised staying calm, and just ambled down from my room, casually saying, 'I'm ready when you are.' He had been chatting to my mother, who asked if we were back together again.

'No,' I said. 'We are just going dancing, nothing more than that. We dance well together and I haven't had anyone to dance with lately.' Mother looked suspicious as we bade her farewell.

Eric was very attentive, holding open the car door, taking my arm, being the gentleman. It seemed as if time had stood still, except that now trust had gone. We got strange looks from friends and acquaintances and, whilst in the powder room, girls asked me if the engagement was on again now that Lynn was off the scene. I just shrugged my shoulders as I applied lipstick, saying, 'We'll see.'

We had a lovely evening, dancing the night away, and I felt free and happy again. Between dances, we sat and drank whilst we talked about my new job and working in London. I felt in control. Then, the band began to play the last smoochy number and the evening was over. We danced one last dance, I collected my coat and went to the car.

Instead of driving straight home, we went to Lovers' Lane, a quiet local spot where couples either cemented or destroyed their relationships. I knew then that Eric expected everything to be the same as it had been before. He kissed me—and I melted. I enjoyed the fondling, and passion almost got out of control, but I knew I must not let that happen. He ran his hand up my leg but I suddenly grabbed it and firmly said 'no'. Being kissed and caressed and touched by him had me struggling with my emotions.

'Come on, you know you still have feelings for me. Let your guard down, give a little.'

With that, I knew what I had to do. I suddenly felt sobered up and pushed him away. 'No Eric, it would never work. I could never trust you again.'

'So you are still cold and frigid, Miss Ice Maiden,' he spat at me.

'Actually,' I retorted, 'I could be warm and passionate, but you destroyed my trust and I can't forget that.'

'Give it time,' he begged. 'We could be good together.'

'Sorry, Eric. I don't think I will ever feel the same way about you again,' I managed to say. 'I love you. I probably will until I find someone else, but the trust is something else, and much harder to accept.'

As I opened the door to get out of the car, he grabbed me and gave me a really warm, passionate kiss, at the same time swearing that he loved me, missed me, wanted to still marry me, and that he'd been stupid to be taken in by Lynn. He begged me to think about it and said he would ring me in a week. I went home to think about what he had said, and I cried for what might have been. For I had made up my mind then and there that I would not go back, and was determined to be strong and get over him.

# CHAPTER **13**
## Epilogue

Finally, at the age of seventeen, I wanted to fly. Not long after starting work at the bank I was invited to join a group of seven girls who had a holiday booked in Italy. One of their friends was now unable to go, so, with the deposit already paid, I was told that if I could get a passport and find the rest of the money, I would be welcome to join them on the trip.

Never having been abroad before, this was a big step for me and I wondered how my parents would react. I was quite surprised—they both considered it an opportunity not to be missed, so the wheels were put in motion. Quite literally, too.

From the minute I was old enough to hold a provisional licence, I had been taking driving lessons. This amused work colleagues, who thought that women shouldn't drive cars. But this was the Sixties, and women were 'burning their bras', becoming independent and fighting for women's rights.

On the day of my driving test, I arrived at the test station full of confidence and followed instructions accordingly. Halfway round the course a ball, followed by a young child, appeared in the middle of the road. I slammed on the brakes so hard and stopped so suddenly that the examiner's notes lay at his feet. I sat wide-eyed and shocked. The mother, now holding the child and his ball at the roadside, was screaming and crying, and almost hysterical.

Having established that the mother and child were both ok, the examiner got back in the car saying, 'I think we can safely dispense with the need to do a further emergency stop! Continue.'

The remainder of the test went like a dream and, although I hit the kerb on my exit from an otherwise successful three-point turn, I passed my driving test. It wasn't long before I had my own car and I became one of the few young women in the town to be a car owner. This had a definite effect on boyfriends, who tended to either shy away or take advantage of my ability to 'go places'. I soon learnt to judge who had what motives!

After two years of commuting to London and its inherent problems—train delays, fare increases, rail strikes—I began to think about working locally again. At the suggestion of a friend who worked as a delivery driver, I applied to her company for a job. That year, I left the bank and joined a solicitors office, but found the work tedious, repetitious and boring. Six months later, I went to work for a car electrical spares company as a delivery driver/shop assistant.

It was an exciting year. I entered the local Carnival Queen competition and was chosen as one of the four attendants; I completed a forty-mile walk from Edmonton to Southend to raise sponsorship for Cancer Relief, accompanied by paratroopers from Aldershot and about one hundred other carnival queens and attendants from the surrounding areas; and I met Bill, and a playboy called Henry...

The doorbell rang, bringing me sharply back to the present, and the table littered with the task I still had to face. I pushed back the chair and went to answer the door, only to discover that it was merely a card pushed through the letterbox. I opened the envelope and read the contents. It was from one of the neighbours who was always the first to deliver her cards, and always as near to the first day of December as possible. Returning to the dining table, I stood the lone Christmas card in front of me, and glanced again into the garden. The plants were blowing in the wind and a misty rain had started to fall as night began to close in, putting the final dismal touch to the day. I thanked my lucky stars that things were different now. I had vowed that once I married, Christmas would not be like those I had lived through and dreaded as a child.

Having received the first card, I felt I had to make a real effort to get this job underway. I decided to be very positive. I had a basic letter composed, which could be amended, altered or added to, depending on who it was being sent to, and edited to suit each individual friend or family member. The whole lot could be gone by the end of the week, of this I was absolutely determined. I always felt a great sense of satisfaction and achievement once the last card was sealed. All I had to do then was to post or distribute them to get them out of the way. Presents that needed to be sent by post were ready, those to be wrapped and put under the tree were well hidden.

As I worked through the list, the cards were piled into neat stacks, with notes attached to indicate which were 'by hand', 'for posting', 'scout post', airmail or for letters to be added. I couldn't help thinking, as I made additional lists of food to buy between now and Christmas, and gifts still to be bought, that all this fuss happened for just two days of celebration. All the extra food, the over-indulgence, the waste produced, was for just two days. Was it all really necessary? Was it worth the worry and effort? Some families would get through it and survive, others would have their dreams shattered and lives wrecked.

The bit I hated most was the complete and utter disruption to normal life. The house would be littered with cards and decorations that got in the way. The whole season was a fiasco. I saw it all as a real commercial rip-off. Everything purchased as a gift in the run-up to Christmas could be purchased a day after as a sale item, or in the ensuing January sales where the items were practically given away.

All the news programmes were disrupted during Christmas and the New Year celebrations. You never knew where to find them, when to expect them, and it was sheer hit and miss to ever be able to get a weather forecast.

The 'Season of Goodwill' is no longer limited to two days either. For most people Christmas is now extended to a week and, in some cases, up to two weeks and even beyond. To my mind, two days was long enough to cause a rift in the family. For some families, two weeks must be a complete and utter nightmare. For those who are elderly and alone, Christmas may well be the worst season of all.

The cards and decorations in our own home will be down on New Year's Day. There is no Twelfth Night tradition for us. New Year's Day seems a much better time. Off with the old and into a new year, with nothing left over from the passing year—except goodwill to all men, women and children for the next three hundred and sixty-five days.